DROPPIN' SEEDS

DROPPIN' SEEDS

A compilation of Spoken Word Poetry for
Grown Folks

Volume 1

Tami P. Thomas-Burton
(aka on stage as "Ol' Skool")

iUniverse, Inc.
New York Lincoln Shanghai

Droppin' Seeds
A compilation of Spoken Word Poetry for Grown Folks

iUniverse books may be ordered through booksellers or by contacting:

iUniverse
2021 Pine Lake Road, Suite 100
Lincoln, NE 68512
www.iuniverse.com
1-800-Authors (1-800-288-4677)

Because of the dynamic nature of the Internet, any Web addresses or links contained in this book may have changed since publication and may no longer be valid.

The views expressed in this work are solely those of the author and do not necessarily reflect the views of the publisher, and the publisher hereby disclaims any responsibility for them.

ISBN: 978-0-595-43388-9 (pbk)
ISBN: 978-0-595-87714-0 (ebk)

Printed in the United States of America

To my Heavenly Father who fashioned me with many gifts and decided that one way I would reach others would be through poetry. You said, "Ask," and I did receive, "Knock," and the doors would open for me, "Seek," and I would find what you had for me. Thank you for your divine inspiration. Much Love & Gratitude from my heart!

&

In Loving memory of my wonderful parents, Leroy Edward and Rogetta (Mimi) Thomas, who were both "Poetry in Motion."
Their positive words, wisdom, laughter, and downright "keep it real" attitudes have allowed me to embrace the feisty freedom and artistic truth telling that flows from my left-handed self to the pen & microphone. Yes, it was through your seed that I was created to be a mouthpiece. Your loquaciousness was a generational gift passed on to me. I love you both deeply.

P.S. Mommy & Daddy, I'll see you again in the life to come.

CONTENTS

Acknowledgements

First and foremost, I would like to thank my sister, Staci M. Thomas-Jackson, who was the 1st to question me on when I would publish my spoken word poetry collection. I thank her for continuously keeping me accountable *(by bugging the heck out of me)* to when it was gonna happen. I love you, "boo-boo"/"boss."

I would like to thank God for the prophetic words given to Pastor Ramona Lewis *(of New Beginnings Church, Aurora, CO).* After a women's conference at Colorado Christian Fellowship *(my church home)* approximately seven years ago, she walked up to me and gave me this message, she said "there are books inside of you, and it's time for you to get busy with doing God's work." Your words were another confirmation, because I knew God had already given me the gifting to write. So here we are, and I thank God for Ramona's obedience and straightforwardness, and I thank God I was able to hear and bear witness with her message.

I would like to thank my three beautiful daughters Ashleigh, Tyler, and Paige who were always the first ears to hear my poetry pieces in draft form. I thank you for your honest yet candid feedback. *(You know kids, they don't lie when given the opportunity & freedom to criticize you on the sly)* It's all good cause I love my little *(they're semi-grown-up)* princesses. Hey, apples don't fall too far away from the tree. What can I say, they're all my little mini-me's!

I like to thank God for placing me in an awesome church home, Colorado Christian Fellowship of Aurora, Colorado. I've been under the leadership of Pastor Phil Smith for eight and half years, and it has been an invaluable experience for me! Pastor Phil, your stewardship, discipline, and passion has taught me a lot about being a fearless soldier for Christ. I truly thank you personally & Thank God for you.

I would like to thank my editor, Judy Howard who had been a great great friend, encourager, and fellow SpeakOut artist. I admire your giftings' and respect your integrity. I'm looking forward to our future projects.

To my three mentors-girlfriends, Nina Hinds, Denita Sconiers, and Aundrey Wilkins, I thank you for that "Iron-sharpens-Iron" thing that we do. Your prayers, long talks, laughter, encouragement, and correction are priceless moments for me. You are the three people in my life that have allowed unguarded moments be memorable. I thank you for seeing the greatness that God has put inside of me.

Speaking of Greatness, I'd like to thank Janemarie Newton for being my awesome life coach. You are so perfect for me! I know girl, I'm a tall order (even though I'm short in stature), but you, over the years have always pressed me and challenged me to new levels of seeing the greatness God has fashioned inside of me. Thank you for being my personal champion who has that "Air Force 1" attitude that you bring. Yeah, white girl! You know this brown girl loves ya!

I would like to thank Karen Thompson for being obedient and bold with the ministry God has given her to oversee. We have known each other for over seven years and have recently grown close as sisters. Karen, without the "SpeakOut," many of these poetic pieces would have either been put on the back burner for years or never written. Participating in the SpeakOut venue since its inception (October 2003) has been another invaluable experience. Thank you sistah for your endurance, unconditional love, and most of all, for being the "lyrical pit-bull" that you are, with your 5 ft? tall self! And remember, I will always be wearing my stiletto's and using some super stiff gel on the top-part of my hair to make myself look a little taller than you. *(Diva Smiles)*

And last, I'd like to thank my SpeakOut Poet Family for the bellyaching laughter, late-late night partying until the wee mornings, your hugs, constructive criticism, our group prayers, and especially for the dance moves you have taught Ol Skool. Thank you Karen Thompson (*aka "Oooh Weee"*), John Thompson (*Our Gig Manager*), Julie Farrow (*Security— "Shug Knight"*), DJ—Curtis Burns (*"C-Note"*), DJ—Star Child (*"Star"*), Alpha Team Lead—Laquetta Farrow (*aka "Puritee"*), Omega Team Lead—Tangela *Ash* (*aka "Sayo/Tan Joy"*), Judy Howard (*aka "The Quickness"*), Clienelle Washington (*aka "What I See"*), Jako Washington (*aka "Did U Learn"*), Pam Ames (*aka "Sho Nuf"*), John Ames (*The After Party Host*), Vicki Harris (*aka "Victory"*), Paige (*aka "Princess Pai"/"Bay Bee Walk"*), Chloe

Rousseau (*aka "Niveah"*), Mandel Rousseau (*aka "Mosaic"*), Ayinde Russell (*aka "De"*), Renetta Price (*aka "Reborn"*), Naye Bullock *("Naye-Naye")*, and Shayla Turner *("Touche")*. Thank you for helping to bring out the authentic poet in me. You have always created a supporting family atmosphere that allowed transparency, creativeness, boldness, integrity and excellence. You are all, *individually,* gifts to me from the Father. I'd also like to acknowledge my other poet friends who occasionally bless us on the mic at the SpeakOut with their gifting's, Anita Mondragon, Meca Littlejohn *("Little Meek"*—yes, this is my name for you!), Primus, Toni Graham, and Calvin Davis *("Cray")*.

PURE PROMISES

One Pure Promise
Is *Growing*
Inside of Me

LET'S GET ACQUAINTED WITH THE PROMISE

Standing in the passage of this vision,
his eyes were gentle,
edged-out like the frames of square sunglasses.
Crystal clear tints,
full of compassion,
and the surety of his gentleness is like,
the skin of a velvet-rose-petal.
Focused on my every move,
and seeing beyond my exterior,
adoration laced his brow
with majesty and unwavering devotion.
This was not some physical attraction,
or the passion of love trapped between two thunderclouds.
He connected to the promise of peaceful places,
so we embraced time standing still.
Then this Loveliness escapes …
and our connection takes over
like needle-pins tingle a sleepy foot.
The snapshot imprints my heart with
a landscaped vision of UTOPIA.
Then, I wake from my slumber
to find myself, waiting, and wanting to
capture the glance of him,
discovering the true promise … OF ME.

Poem:　　　　　　*Let's Get Acquainted with the Promise*

Inspiration:	*Written 05/20/06*
Annotations:	*This is a love poem, and is about how the eyes are the windows to the soul.*
Dedications:	*I dedicate this poem to myself. Its inspiration comes from a night dream God gave me.*
Truth Meditations:	<u>*Psalms 12:6*</u> *"The words and promises of the Lord are pure words, like silver refined in an earthen furnace, purified seven times over."*
	<u>*Matthew 6:22-23*</u> *"The eye is the lamp of the body. If your eyes are good, your whole body will be full of light. But if your eyes are bad, your whole body will be full of darkness. If then the light within you is darkness, how great is that darkness?*
Contemplations:	*Ask Yourself* ➔ *Everything else aside, does the reflection of this poem resonate with you? If so, how?*
	Ask Yourself ➔ *Are you willing to close the door when it should be slammed closed?*
	Ask Yourself ➔ *When someone looks in your eyes, what are you certain they will see?*

MULTITUDES OF LOVE

Love at the Mountain Top
Love at the Valley Low
To Do
Or
Not to do
That is the Answer!
Not the Question!
Not the Confusion.
Not the Worldly amusement,
Of life's roller coaster rides.
Because Love at the top & valley low
Is
His Love.
Tough Love.
Sweet Love.
His never leaving you Love.
Just Lov'n to
Embrace His gentle presence.
Just Be'n
To Be
In Love with Thee.
You see,
Before I can Love,
I need to hug Him & all that's inside of me.
The instant familiar is often a trick.
Is this trick or treat?
Liking me & Loving myself are two different things.
I see candy apple lies....
And not the sweet smell'n truth.
But!

Those invisible kisses you give me,

And you hold me all—day—long.

My heavenly husband,

My cry, giggles, and attitude you patiently entertain.

The clay of my ways you earnestly shape.

Teaching me to unlearn.

Steering my longings.

Pushing my passions.

Stopping my guilt.

Fighting my Fears with me.

I love you friend.

You are here.

You are near.

Here for me.

Loving me,

On the Mountain top,

& the Valley low.

My maker, my navigator, my friend.

I reach for you.

I long for you.

You are mine.

You are Multitudes of Love.

Poem:	*Multitudes of Love*
Inspiration:	*Written on 10/02/03*
Annotations:	*This is an expression of my love for my Heavenly Father in spite of the adversities I've experienced in my life.*

Truth Meditation: *God is Love.* <u>*Deuteronomy 6:5*</u> *"Love the Lord your God with all your heart and with all your soul and with all your strength."*

Contemplations: *Ask Yourself* ➔ *What stands in your way of having a life full of passion?*

Ask Yourself ➔ *What stands in your way of having all the love you desire?*

REVITALIZE

Revitalize, Focus, Hear, to be heard,

By the Angles in heaven and the Father above.

Collecting my prayers,

Heavens' walls part

From the green and blue canvas in which I live.

But my inner ear hears it's all in the Master's hand.

His hand, His feet, His Plan,

Is why I retreat

To realign my walk again.

Major turns & minor detours.

I trust the voice that navigates,

On the road to relocation,

I don't pack a box,

I just sit still and wait.

Still & quiet, He whispers my next steps.

Stop, pause, listen, receive, plant, water,

The message the Maker makes.

In Heaven above, the time is yesterday, today, and tomorrow.

As the clock counts,

Faith is the formula and Work removes fear and doubt.

Mt. Fear brings tears,

Mt. Doubt gets you off route.

I'm here and want to stay on track,

Your Will, Your Way, Your Stack….

Of Promises,

I want to receive,

I retreat to revitalize and focus with ease.

I welcome Your wisdom and die for the cause.

Help me to continue in the direction of the light.

Your yoke is easy, and Your arms have all might.

Revitalize, Focus, hear to be heard,
The cycle of Love is all in the God's Word.
Please help me to pause,
Because there is a cause,
I want to trust your loving whisper
As I, Revitalize.

Poem:	*Revitalize*
Inspiration:	*written 06/04/03*
Annotations:	*I wrote this piece thinking that it is good to retreat and refuel the places that only God can fill.*
Dedications:	*I dedicate this poem to my dad who lived life to the fullest. His life has continuously reminded me that even when it's full of "wonderful" and "easy," only the Father in Heaven can ground me in true peace and comfort.*
Meditation:	*<u>Philippians 4:7</u> "And the peace of God, which passeth all understanding, shall keep your hearts and minds through Christ Jesus."*
	<u>Matthew 6:6</u> "But when you pray, go into your room, close the door and pray to your Father, who is unseen. Then your Father, who sees what is done in secret, will reward you."
Contemplations:	*Ask Yourself → Who's voice is getting in the way of your peace and joy?*
	Ask Yourself → What will a change in attitude create in your life?
	Ask Yourself → If there was only one thing you could do that you haven't done yet, what would that be & what guidance will you search for to support your goal?

HE DESIRES HER

His Prayers are all about who she is,
this missing part of this rib of his.
He desires a warm, loving, supportive woman.
A woman who is intelligent, respectful, energetic, laughs,
and genuinely loves life,
a life without nagging or strife.
He desires her,
a woman who loves attention, touch, kisses, going places, adventure,
her blend of friends,
and watching her through his social lens.
He desires her,
Who he can send thoughtful words of encouragement,
just because he's thinking of her brilliance and amazing resilience.
He loves her miles away, by putting a smile on her body part,
Yes!, he knows the abstract art of sending kisses to her heart.
He desires her,
whom he can romance,
hold hands and date for the rest of his life,
all the sprinkles of wrinkles, and grey hairs that crinkle.
He desires her,
a woman of the same faith, similar values,
recognizable ethics, and established morals.
He desires her,
and loves her children, God-children,
adopted, foster, and natural ones too.
He is fully aware that she is female,
the feminine part of man
whose purpose is to receive,
nurture, cleave, and support him like Adam's wife Eve.
He desires her,

a partner with integrity,
prepared and grown-up for him,
one that will be there sink or swim,
because of her,
he's eager to workout at the gym,
dunk'n rims, stay'n trim, healthy, and slim,
yes she's the only one for him.
He desires her,
his soul-mate whom he can trust,
share his fears, dreams, faith, and unexpected detours,
because their unbroken suture of love will always endure.
He desires her,
as his other half who understands
prosperity, prayer, and provision,
his leadership decisions,
Godly visions,
and his covenant with circumcision.
He desires her,
as pure, secure, and mature.
His wife, lover, friend, and business mate,
one he'll serve, protect and sacrifice for a zero exchange rate.
He desires her
to be in agreement with him as they excel in life as one,
accomplishing all of their individual goals
singing, "we've only just begun."
He desires her,
the strong independent confident partner
who cherishes her time alone,
to stay in her zone,
yet values their intimate time alone.
He desires her,

the woman who's inner, outer, and mental world stimulates
    complements,
intellectual conversations,
and loving words of truth,
springing forth like the fountain of youth,
free from flatter or needless chatter.
He desires her,
a partner for life
who's forever focused on her beauty & health,
and God's prescribed Kingdom of wealth.
He desires her
because he finds beauty in her personality-voice,
the way she eats,
her appetite for World Peace,
and how her temper ceases to ever increase.
He desires her
and knows that his words are nothing but a wishbone
without the heavenly Father's throne.
Yes, he's wanting the full-package,
and not the plastic clone.
So, he preserves his loins
with self-control and faith,
trusting the Pearly White Gates,
he boldly awaits Heavens timing to be great,
and at the heart of his fire for desire.
Because, He Desires Her.

Poem: *He Desires Her*

Inspiration: *written 04/28/98*

Annotations:	*I wrote this from the female romantic perspective and what I think most women think men want in a true, loving, God-appointed relationship.*
Dedications:	*I dedicate this to every man and woman who are in love, engaged to be married, and know the purpose of their union.*
Meditation:	*Proverbs 18:22 "He who finds a true wife finds a good thing and obtains favor from the Lord."*
Contemplations:	*Ask Yourself → Is there more to be discovered about you?*
	Ask Yourself → How would others describe you?
	Ask Yourself → How would you describe (in a non-religious way) how God sees you?

LOVE,
LESSONS,
& GROUNDINGS

Love,
Lessons,
and *Groundings*
are the Ingredients to
digging up Truth

I'M HERE, BACK HOME!

It's quiet in my spirit, … a peaceful quiet is all around me,
yet life's voices muffle the air.
There are big mountains that surround my inner and outer world.
What a mess I've chosen!
You know … I'm not running, I just want the lesson to end.
Surrounded by heaven's brown hues of creation,
in my thoughts, in my eyes, in the subconscious layers of my skin.
God, you made us so uniquely rich in you.
Ahh! Back Home!
Back Home!
I've been out in some Ghetto-Oz-land,
wanting to click my runned-down shoes back to my mansion.
Back home to my real spiritual place.
This…. "kind," "gullible," "nice-crap,"
I don't find appealing about myself anymore.
It just attracts the wounded, weak, and full-of baggage type fools.
Father, you've brought me to a different world of awareness,
on a different plane of insight.
God I obviously didn't know how to self-love deeply,
Otherwise I wouldn't be here fighting for my life.
Skills on the outside, tears on the inside.
Swimming on the outside, Drowning on the inside.
You know, my choices have been based on reactive selfish love.
I look around and I see all my brothers and sister, your children Lord.
Some loving themselves deeply, nurturing their spirits, and some not!
I can see it in their eyes like ornamented lifeless pines.
Just touch their fragileness, and thousands of needles fall like
    generations of tears.
I care for them as much as I do me.

Father, you planted omniposcence all around me, in me, and through me.

My lessons have had many quizzes, study sessions, and misunderstandings as well.

I've paid the price of "drama" painted the hue of "stupidity."

Lived like a junk-yard dog.

No money, no class, no real love in my life.

Mind wars, Spiritual battles, and emotional torture.

But you Lord, heard the echo of my cry, and I have so, so, so much gratitude.

Tough love, Tough Lessons, as you painfully watched, yet you held me.

And now I know, there's room for only mountains that I climb with you.

I love myself & I'm here.

I hear you, Spirit of God.

I'm here!

Back Home!

Rest, Peace, Laughter, Smiles, Joy.

I'm on the new pages of my journey.

I'm here, Back Home!

❧ ❧ ❧ ❧ ❧ ❧ ❧ ❧ ❧ ❧ ❧ ❧

Poem:	*I'm Here, Back Home*
Inspiration:	*Coming out of a crazy! crazy! crazy! second marriage. I guess I was crazy to say yes at the alter. It was two horrible years, but I learned volumes about myself.*
Annotations:	*Everything has a Season … and sometimes people are in your life for a season.*
Dedications:	*To "new beginnings" after divorce.*
Meditation:	*Isaiah 40:9 "Get thee up into the high mountains."*

John 16:33 "These things I have spoken unto you, that in me ye might have peace. In the world ye shall have tribulation: but be of good cheer; I have overcome the world.

Contemplations: *Ask Yourself* ➔ What overpowers you?

Ask Yourself ➔ On a scale from 1 to 10, where does your "inward fight" fall in overcoming the things you know you need to.?

Ask Yourself ➔ Like Dorothy in the Wizard of Oz, where would you like to click your heel home to?

BE REAL, BROTHA

You See,
You look good, smell good, and taste good too,
But is that the real you?

I know the real you frowns when you're dead-dog sick,
has stinky breath when you wake, and a temper that's quick!
The real you is salty when you sweat from hard work,
and last year, you looked good, smelled good, and taste good too,
But now I know, that ain't the real you.

Your words to my ear tickled my female parts,
You held my hand and made me laugh,
Loved me, caressed me, like I was all that.

Is this the real you?
Be real, because I'm lov'n all that's "this" and all that's "that."
But some how, the real you is smelling like a musty rat.

You See,
Your words got stale, and the tickle became a tick,
That itched my ears and bothered my wit.

I feel like shaking your hand good-bye instead of stroking my message.
Your love is cold, mechanical & dull,
And this cat-dog chase is like poison in that cross bone skull.

You use to honor me as your Queen.
Talk to me, talk with me and ponder the wisdom of my youth.
I saw you watching me and studying me as you counted your loot.

But is that the real you?
Hell No!

Because now you honor me with commands, demands, and high
hands.

And now the queen quilts a picture of unhappy quilt.

And now I'm begg'n you to "talk to me," "talk to me,"
But you ignore me & snore for me.
And my wisdom never gets in,
Because your wet dreams are your stolen fantasy's and your secret sins.

Now!
Your Daydreams are your nightmares,
And your Night-Dreams are your day stares.
Glares, Stares, Glances, Fantasies, and Lust,
Is the web you caught me in at that false-date with trust.

Now, the lesson is over, and I know how to see real.
And real is not what you are.
It's not how you taste, smell, or how you feel,
It's about how bright your heart shines like that very distant star.

This journey with you was a hypnotic trick.
Dogs do tricks,
And real men never get the gold that quick.
Be Real & Really Be!, that man that God intended for me to see.
The real journey should unfold and not be trick cards out of a hat.
And what I see, feel & know,
I really want to be all that!
Be Real Brothers.

Poem:	*"Be Real Brotha"*
Inspiration:	*written 03/08/02*

Annotations:	*I wrote this reflection after coming out of an extremely unpleasant ("ghetto fabulous") short-lived 2nd marriage. Marriage is not a game, so know thyself!*
Dedication:	*To every "testosterone-occupied-male-species" in this world.*
Meditation:	*I John 2:15-16 "Do not love the world or anything in the world. If anyone loves the world, the love of the Father is not in him. For everything in the world—the cravings of sinful man, the lust of his eyes and the boasting of what he has and does—comes not from the Father but from the world."*
	I John 1:8 "If we say that we have no sin, we deceive ourselves, and the truth is not in us."
	James 1:22 "But be ye doers of the word, and not hearers only, deceiving your own selves."
Contemplations:	*Ask Yourself* → *Are you living your life or is someone else's?*
	Ask Yourself → *Are your choices based on your values or desires?*

I'M CHECKIN' YOU OUT!

I already know that you skin is walnut brown,

And the bumps in your wallet and the bumps on your arms are thick
     and hard,

Solid like a fat pomegranate.

Juicy full lips, You know you're fine.

Even your scent is familiar.

But you see,

I'm checkin' out your spirit!

So, why don't you turn around for me,

Your blind side need my view.

Hmmm, Nice.

I see you rest in your decisions and that you trust God.

Very Nice.

Now bend over, I need to check out this view too.

Uhm, Very Nice.

Oh, for me brother? Nice choice of flowers,

You picked lily's from the garden of Eden.

Uhm! A spirit of gratitude for the common things in life.

Very Nice.

Brother, have a seat, relax, lay back, kick your feet up!

Interesting!

Your body is vertical, but your thoughts are horizontal & parallel with
     the heavens.

Oh, you want to talk,

Talk about our Maker, our God, and the voice on the inside.

Nice! Very Nice!

Uhm! … well how about some movement now?

Brother, would you like to dance with me?

Or would you like to dance for me?
Or would you like to prance on me?
Oh!, so you're a brother that loves to read and read out loud.
What does that have to do with dancing?
So, that's how you dance!
That's how your move to your music, through the pages.
Nice! Very Nice!

Brother how about a drink?
Would you like a glass of wine?
Sure my sister, I will join you for a walk.
A walk! You want to walk with me?
Yes sister, let's relax and walk in the vineyard.
So tell me, what's on your mind?
What do you meditate on?
What's your favorite color?
Are you tickle-ish?
Wow your eyes are beautiful and clear.
Your hands are like your mother and your will is like your father.
Your have a mole on your neck.
Sister, look there's a lightening bug.
Can I walk with you again?
Sister, I've enjoyed these fine glasses of wine you have offered me.

Well Brother, the night is young and I'm a little tired.
Would you like to massage my shoulders and neck please?
Sure my sister, my hands have worked hard today,
And all I have to offer is a handshake of my friendship.

Uhm! That was nice.
And you know, the scent of his spirit has left an aroma in my house.
There's more to the journey,
But the question becomes, who's checkin' who?

Poem:	*I'm Checkin' You Out!*
Inspiration:	*written 02/08/02*
Annotations:	*Dating is more than attraction. Our culture teaches us to win each other over. See, I've learned that relationships are more than chemistry and attraction. God made us as three parts, body, mind, and spirit. So, make sure all three are on the one accord.*
Dedications:	*To single people desiring a mate.*
Meditation:	*Proverb 27:7 "he full soul loatheth an honeycomb; but to the hungry soul every bitter thing is sweet.*
	Romans 8:5 "For they that are after the flesh do mind the things of the flesh; but they that are after the Spirit the things of the Spirit."
Contemplations:	*Ask Yourself → What does chemistry versus heart connections mean to you?*
	Ask Yourself → What's important to you in a relationship?
	Ask Yourself → What qualities in relationships are lasting to you?

CRIMINAL CONVERSATION

You see, you know you off limits
when you speak a hello to sister girl,
followed by that grin-type smile,
swipe'n your tongue against your lips,
with a quick glance at her hips,
knowing that you have a woman at home
in grips of your paycheck,
your sperm,
your secrets,
and all the assets of your business firm.

But you still wanted to touch the stove,
knowing you gonna get burned.
Brother let me tell you,
you just had a "criminal conversation"
with a female fantasy of your fascination.
But you choose to leave your fingerprints
with a "hello"
echoing subliminal undertones of
"ooh baby,"
"what's your name?"
AND
"Uh! Uh! Umm!"

Now I see that
you didn't see that
at one time
your words were treasures in my jewelry box,
the one with the little ballerina dancing on top.
See I had tiptoe experiences with you
even minus the orgasms and giggles

that stretched my stomach to the hurting point.
Those baby pink moments
remind me of blowing bubbles,
skip'n backwards,
and holding hands in the breeze of the night.
Yeah, you touched it!....
knowing that at some point
the oven door would drop down on
the trueness of how a little yeast
would still spoil the leaven of all this ...
FRESH.... BAKED.... BROWN.... BISCUIT!

I ain't Finish!
But you decided
to have a criminal conversation
with another woman,
forgetting that the heartbeat of you
as a helpmate was just one phone call away,
today,
yesterday,
as a matter fact,
everyday is the proper way to say
that you "high rolling,"
"chance taking," self
lost your prosperity in a snap,
when you opened the door to "lack of trust!"

It's crime that
you choose "Ms. green apple bootie"
versus stick'n with
the "Sweet Pomegranate beauty."
Your teeth choose to dig for 2 seeds
versus the 99

that always exceeded you capacity to finish
before moaning "Oh my God!"
you know what I mean.
Um huh, yeah, she's cute,
but I'm smart and fine.
She's lost in herself,
and I'm a 1962 Zinfandel Cherry Wine.
And don't you forget,
the blacker the berry the sweeter the juice.
But you chose to brand adultery on us,
on our intimate conversations,
on our plans to leave fingerprints on nations,
the promise of procreation to our parents.
You cheated! Not me.

So, now
I look back
and wisdoms message has taught that
we entered in,
blowing the purity vow,
a defiled bed,
didn't know how to tap into longevity's juice
called "until death do us part"
requiring us to have hearts of unconditional love,
unmoved by distractions,
and painting the work of art called
God's word
over all our territories.
We were young rabbits,
hopping to the beat of EveryReady,
the blue hypnotics of

lust, laughter, and comfort zones,
covering the rust *of us* not knowing ourselves.

And so today,
I realize I should of told you "NO"
with your super-fine self.
I should of said backup,
and my kisses should have been pecks
instead of lots of saliva exchange.
Those class rings on necks
should have only been dating strings
and not those covenant-type things.
But I let you into my world
of diamonds, rubies, and pearls,
when you had ready whispering softly
all that my female ears wanted to hear.

So my confession is.... yeah,
you temporarily broke my heart,
but now, *(sing)* "the thrill is gone!"
Your criminal acts
have violated my values, ethics and my core.
And another thing,
save yourself a trip to the store,
cause I ain't giving you the ring back either.

See, I've learned to love myself fully.
I refuse to be sweet talked into
going with the flow,
being mesmerized by your doe,
or breath taking appearance.

So, to the next brother,
just know that I am wait'n

for the one conversation that God brings,

and if you ain't in that discussion,

we can be casual friends,

but you ain't the one

that's suppose to have this precious stone.

♣ ♣ ♣ ♣ ♣ ♣ ♣ ♣ ♣ ♣ ♣ ♣

Poem:	*Criminal Conversation*
Inspiration:	*written 06/21/06*
Annotations:	*This piece is a reflection of my past, my lessons around setting boundaries, self-love, and my lack of wisdom as a young person in the dating arena. Writing this poem has helped me to heal from the betrayal.*
Dedications:	*To my 1st boyfriend, my 1st love in high school who broke my heart years ago. You are such a wonderful person, but Babe, "it is what it is" & "it beez what it beez."* *Thou shalt not cheat on the one you love.*
Meditation:	*Exodus 20:14 "Thou shalt not commit adultery."*
	I Corinthians 6:13-19 "Food for the stomach and the stomach for food"—but God will destroy them both. The body is not meant for sexual immorality, but for the Lord, and the Lord for the body. By his power God raised the Lord from the dead, and he will raise us also. Do you not know that your bodies are members of Christ himself? Shall I then take the members of Christ and unite them with a prostitute? Never! Do you not know that he who unites himself with a prostitute is one with her in body? For it is said, "The two will become one flesh." But he who unites himself with the Lord is one with him in spirit. Flee from sexual immorality. All other sins a man commits are outside his body, but he who sins sexually sins against his own body. Do you not know that your body is a temple of

the Holy Spirit, who is in you, whom you have received from God? You are not your own;"

Contemplations:

Ask Yourself ➜ What keeps you from saying no when you know you should?

Ask Yourself ➜ What will saying "no" do to you?

Ask Yourself ➜ What is your filter for the choices you make?

GHETTO HELL

I'm talk'n bout,
HELL painted the hue of smoky confusion,
fal-set-to noise,
the stench of lies
try'n to creep up my Stiletto's and thighs,
keep'n me walk'n the streets,
as I fight and swing my fist
to the beat of Ghetto Hell.
There ain't no strut'n,
I want to run like hell from this prison,
but it's keep'n me from saying farewell.
My brain cells ache
as I dwell in this frail sleep-deprived body,
smell'n like the incense of a funeral home.
But I tell you,
I must escape this Hell,
it's a mapped-out generational trap
to "exist for" or "die in."
And I'm wait'n for some school bell
to snap wake me out of this nightmare.
Looks like a sleepwalking trance,
glancing at zombies and super humans
in a different state of mind,
dancing to enhance the romance
with the snake's game of take a change.
My head is spinning and drained
from fight'n my vocals
to keep it from shoot'n me down
with these brainwashed locals.
I sleep from deep exhaustion

and wake-up tired from night sweats
of worry and blurry heartaches.
My tears dehydrate my underbody
with salt less sweat of this somebody,
mutated, disgusted, and rated with hatred
by the lustful lover,
Evil himself.
But nobody cares
about the weeping despair of my internal life.
Cast-iron knots in my stomach,
you can't rescue me from this dark drama.... Mama!
Only some divine intervention
will kill this curse
without bruising me,
loosing me,
or confusing me with false hope.
My oozing cry
screams-silently for help.
But somehow I'm suddenly numb from feeling
and pause to accept my killing foolishness.
Will I repeat the lesson?
I yell silently,
HELL NO! & No to Hell!
I've been grounded to smell the roses,
thorns and all.
My shout gurgles
with a mouthwash of my own sweat and blood.
Gums bleeding
to grit and bear the pain of
being lost in my own wilderness.
Panting short to my heartbeat,
lungs half full,

I close my eyes
and see specks of silver glitter
in the black and blueness
of my squinting hard…. and expecting.

But now, I become clear with spears of adrenaline
shooting my shaking hands,
to reach for the light.
I smell the dryness of the wilderness
burn my noise like below-zero air.
Epiphany's glare shows me to
seek the peace I knew.
So, I earnestly reach for some smiling cheeks of truth.
I knock and preach to the fresh water creeks,
I see the moisture of grateful and meek I knew.
I seek and I'm given Wisdoms technique
of not repeating the lesson.

It was a Ghetto Hell!
I've been there, done that!
And I ain't repeat'n the lesson!

Poem:	*GHETTO HELL*
Inspiration:	*written 03/11/06*
Annotations:	*Reflections on a Ghetto-Hell-relationship I survived. And I thank God I escaped and learned a lot about myself.*
Dedications:	*To all the women in the world who have been in abusive relationships and have found a way out and have learned what you needed to learn from that experience about yourself. Not about him, but about yourself.*

Meditation:

Romans 8:28 "*and we know that all things work together for good to them that love God, to them who are the called according to his purpose.*"

Ezekiel 23:49 "*And they shall recompense your lewdness upon you, and ye shall bear the sins of your idols: and ye shall know that I am the Lord GOD.*"

Contemplations:

Ask Yourself ➔ *Are you in a Ghetto Hell? If so, Why?*

Ask Yourself ➔ *What keep you out of a dramatic situations?*

Ask Yourself ➔ *Describe your lifestyle and decide if it's pleasant or unpleasant?*

REAL LIFE
UNCENSORED

Real Life Uncensored
is keeping me *Fertilized* with
Warnings,
Wisdom,
and
Understanding

WHAT ELSE COULD BE TRUE ABOUT YOU?

(SCENE 1)

When I feel like full swing slapp'n you, I have to violently pause and do a little chromosome mapp'n of you, and "sweat-hope" that my hands might be clapp'n for you. Lord, help me to the promise land as I fight for this, cause I really want to leave some blue and black marks on you. See I'm so pissed, I want to reenact that clench-fist scene in the "Color Purple," but I'm at work, and I can't go out that way ... hand-cuffed that is! So, I unlock my jaws and take a deep breath.... and my open-eyes examine you X-ray and see that your genetic design is not as pathetic as I celebrated. And in that instance, truth meets my knower, in a flicker of an eye. ME.... catching my breath instead slips into greeting your neck with a Peace-sign rope in forgiveness, yet laced in my dried-up perspiration.

Yeah, I'm glad I Paused ... think'n ... what else could be true about you?

Perhaps in these moments of time, I don't rely on what's factual, but what could be a contract to love instead of hate, a contract to pray ... instead of words the create debate. A contract to turn the other cheek and speak words of kindness that show my color-blindness. Perhaps in these situations, I don't rely on what's real, but what my spirit-heart feels.

(SCENE 2)

When I feel like battling your ideas and arguing to win, I have to violently pause, remembering that I have flaws too. And going to that ghetto-land of "Oz" ain't noth'n but the devils jaws clapp'n and flapp'n us around like puppets on his string. Yeah, I fell into the temptation of bringing you words that feels like bee strings just to win, but I notice the kids are receiving the venom from our body language. So, I pause to help myself grow into my wholeness ad well-roundedness ... hips, heart, thighs and all. See, deep down, I really want to bring the sur-real-type things, words that take on a lifespan like Martin Luther King. Wrestling my tongue against your in this lyrical boxing ring, keeps me from hearing your articulation of debate ... iced in cherry-top wisdom that I discounted for the price tag of a blue-light sale at K-mart. Honey, forgive me, I'm sorry.

Yeah, I'm glad I Paused ... think'n ... what else could be true about you?

Perhaps I these moments of time, I don't rely on what's black and white, but what's colorful and right. A commitment to engage in expecting daily reparations of bread & red-wine manna that feeds my soul-heart with the fruit of self-control. My goal, to-not stumble in cosmic black holes, sucking me into infernal ugliness painted the hue of lethal stupidity. I want to stay "un-dizzy" in this busy calling on my life. And at these moments in time, I pause for the cause, and long to be free to experience the truth of love from above … instead.

Yeah, I'm glad I Paused!

♣ ♣ ♣ ♣ ♣ ♣ ♣ ♣ ♣ ♣ ♣ ♣

Poem:	*What else could be true about you?*
Inspiration:	*written 04/03/06*
Annotations:	*I was inspired to write this because of all the un-loveable people I've either experienced at work, home, church, or in my personal life.*
Dedications:	*This is dedicated to all the people in my life who have pushed my buttons in the wrong way, I thank you for helping me to pause.*
Meditation:	*Colossians 3:12-14 "Therefore as God's chosen people, holy and dearly loved, clothe yourself with compassion, kindness, humility, gentleness and patience. Bear with each other and forgive whatever grievance you may have against one another. Forgive as the Lord forgave you."*
Contemplations:	*Ask Yourself* → *How does lashing-out at a foolish person serve you?*
	Ask Yourself → *Do you have a short fuse or long one? And Why?*
	Ask Yourself → *How do you deal with difficult people?*

SLEEP WALK'N

HEARTBEAT MOV'N TO THIS PLACES BEAT
AND THE RACE OF THIS GAME CALLED "SIN CITY."
ITS RHYTHM TO KEEP ME ZOMBIEFIED
WITH FLASHING LIGHTS & BIG GLITTER.
THE SMELL OF HUMIDITY SWEAT,
AND THE FUNKY PERFUME OF NIGHT CLUB'N,
SMOKE & FOG-FREE,
BUT THE THICKNESS OF ITS LURE
TO GRAB MY CONSCIOUS,
WALK'N DEAD,
EYES PLASTERED WIDE-OPEN.
SEE YOU NEVER BLINK,
12 HOURS LATER,
BUT ITS WINK SUDUCES ME
IN THE POPPYFIELDS OF SUBLINMINAL WORLDS
LACED LIKE THE STUFF THAT LOOKS LIKE
POWERED SUGAR MINUS THE SWEET,
AND HOW ROCK-SALT LACES THE GLASS
OF A VIRGIN MARGARITA.
MISTER SENOR,
AND ALL YOU MAMA-CITA'S,
NEGRO-RITA'S,
ASIA-NITA'S,
AND CAUCASIA-NITA'S!
... NOTHING BUT A RAINBOW COALITION
OF THE SPECIES CALLED "VEGAS ANT FARM!"
BIRDS-EYE VIEW,
WHEN I COUNT TO THREE,
1, 2, 3!
I NEED SNAP-WAKE YOU

OUT OF THIS HYPNOTIC TRANCE.
IF THE CURE FOR THE ITCH
WAS ONLY A DOSE OF CHAMOMILE,
A SOFT PINK COMA TO
ELECTROSHOCK YOU BACK
INTO YOUR PLACE OF KINGDOM COMES
AND THY WILL BE DONE.
INSTEAD OF COYOTE UGLY,
TEQUILA SHOTS,
LOTTERY TICKETS,
SLOT MACHINES,
CHING-CHING,
ANOTHER GRAND SLIPS OUT MY HAND,
HORSE BETS,
POKER TABLES,
AND RUSSIAN ROULET'S.
6-BARREL GUN, WITH....
1 BULLET, 1 CHANCE, 1 DELIVERANCE,
AND 1 GLANCE AT "HOPE-DISTORTED!"

WAKE-UP! … FROM YOUR SLEEPWALKING!!!
YOU'VE BLOCKED-OUT TRUTHS TREASURE
AND THE REAL FORTUNE
CALLED EVERLASTING WEALTH.

YOUR WIFE, KIDS, HUSBAND, AND SELF
HAVE SUFFERED FROM THE STENCH
OF DEAD THAT LINGERS FROM YOUR THIRSTY HABIT.
I CAN ONLY PRAY THAT
YOU DON'T TRIP ON THE ROCKS & STONES
IN THESE PLACES,
AND DECEPTION LOOSES THE PACE
OF EVIL-KANIVALS RACE.

YOU WALK THE STRIP,
WATCH THE NEON BILLBOARD
TRY TO MIMIC THE RED-YELLOW SUN.
AND ITS COLORFUL DISTRACTION
IS NUMBING YOU WITH BELLYACHES OF DRUNK
    LAUGHTER.
SEE, THE "TRUTH-GIVER" MIGHT COME
IN A BLINK OF AN EYE, AND....
12 HOURS LATER,
WILL YOUR EYES BE PLASTERED WIDE-OPEN
LIKE A SLEEP WALK'N ZOMBIE?

Poem:	*Sleep Walk'n*
Inspiration:	*written: 08/18/06*
Annotations:	*I wrote this waiting to board my airplane in the Las Vegas Airport. I had spent a few days on the strip vacationing, and I learned that we should never be brought under the control or power of anything other than the reign of Christ in our lives.*
Dedications:	*To any person who is or has been or is addicted to Gambling. This is a warning to you!*
Meditation:	*I Corinthians 10:23 "Everything is permissible but not everything is constructive."*
	John 14:1-4 "Do not let your hearts be troubled. Trust in God; trust also in me. In my Father's house are many rooms; if it were not so, I would have told you. I am going there to prepare a place for you. And if I go and prepare a place for you, I will come back and take you to be with me that you also may be where I am. You know the way to the place where I am going."
Contemplations:	*Ask Yourself* → *What does success look like to you?*

Ask Yourself ➔ *What does failure look like to you?*

Ask Yourself ➔ *What do you think about the statement,
"People live to eat, poop, and die!" Your thoughts?*

KISS'N UP IS HARD TO DO

Part 1

It takes two participants to bend down and stoop to the Office Politics of Kiss'n up.
You see, It's tough, and if you don't believe me, just listen up.

You see, there's…. a…. Greater & Lesser Love Affair going on between a "Control Freak" and the one standing "Naked and Meek."

There's 2-Agenda's to be accomplished,
one is to cover ones fears, and the other is to beg their way … while holding back tears.

Pucker your lips because climbing the Corporate Ladder; you have to wear your Dr. Jekyll & Mr. Hyde Mask. Stabbing people in the back as you take credit for all their tasks. Jump'n hoops, back-flips, & cartwheels for the sake of a raise. Your 8-hours must seem like 30 stressful days. You're in the human food-chain of survival of the fittest, Wimps finish last, and Bullies just finish. The Boss says, the fate of your career is in my hands, so your promotion is nothing but in quicksand. Sounds like somebody's try'n to play-god with my questionable job.

This vicious race is destroying my pace, and tying my hands with rubber bands. I'm not progressing down the road promised to me. I see the yellow brick road to the land of "OZ-Ought" to be my own boss. Nobody's tossing me to & fro. Besides, you can't pay me what I'm really worth in doe. So, brush your nails off, cause people-pleasing is out of style. Stand-up! Be a Leader of Excellence! And run that good mile!

[CAUSE … KISS'N UP IS HARD TO DO!] *(sing melody)*

Part 2

It takes two participants to bend down and stoop to the religious church politics of Kiss'n up.

You see, there's a Greater and Lesser love affair going on between Mr. or Ms. Holier-than-thou and "A Servant" ... Oh, I mean "Slave."

Yeah I said it! sorry my friend, you don't have it made in the shade ... You're just a Cave-Man type Slave. And you just gave and gave and gave ... your time show'n up at every event, you even gave up pizza, ribs and coffee, for Good Friday and Lent. Try'n to please the Pastor, the Preacher, Minister, and Teacher, the Elder, Deacon, Bishop, Priest, Apostle, Greeter and the Prophet, Good Lord Almighty! ... Just Stop-it! *Ain't your lip tired of puckering up?* ... try'n to earn your way to the pulpit stage? Trust me, this only leads to that Postal-type Rage.

There's 2-Agenda to be accomplished,
one is to cover ones fears, and the other is to work for seven unlucky years.

You say 7 years, that's what Jacob in the bible did right? Wrong story, wrong situation, to this application. Listen Buddy, honey, sweetheart, who ever you are, All that you do in church should be out of love for your Maker, and not the Pulpit-Shaker. This reality TV show is called,
"Church-Leaders Behaving Badly," And "Flunkies Following Sadly," And "Spectators laughing Madly." It's a sleepwalking trap.... so snap out of it! Playing church is a waste of time, Serve your God with your own Rhythm & Rhyme.

[CAUSE ... KISS'N UP IS HARD TO DO!] *(sing melody)*

Part 3

It takes two participants to bend down and stoop to the Pro-Athlete Kiss'n Up.

You see there's a Greater & Lesser Love Affair going on between "Mr. Rich over Night" and a "Greedy Groupie."

Picture this, he smiles in front of the masses of fans, But he's longing for you to scream ... "Baby, You-da—Man." Then he says let's go to the hotel, so I can see your tan, and if you got skills with a fry'n pan ... Jan! ... Oh, your names not Jan *(my bet)*, It's Barbie? Are you Fashion Barbie, Hooker Barbie, wanting to become Princess Barbie? Or maybe you're Vintage Barbie, because it's a new season and the toy collector need a new doll, trust me, he has his reasons. He's "Gigolo-Jock" with jock-itch and who knows what else, but you're his fox, so he says let's rock. Girrrl, don't party to be a part of a "Hoochie-Heirum." Trust me, it not your ticket to freedom and Star-dum. Dream'n, Wish'n, Want'n, "to be" through the eyes of another you see, ain't cutt'n it for me. Trapped with gifts like diamonds and silk, and he reminds you, "Girl, without me, you ain't nothing but cornflakes without the milk."

There's 2-Agenda's to be accomplished here, one is to cover ones fears *(of loosing his contract)* and the other is to "work it Girl! ... cause baby-got-back."

Girl, trade your dark circled eyes & your anorexic self in. Because your worth more than that hoochie-girl pen. Barbie—In—Wonder—Land ... wake up!.... Your falling down a hole of wondering if you're the next to be cut. Don't let this take a toll on your soul. A dose of Self-Confidence will have you Strut'n your stuff. Just walk away and say you've had enough!

[CAUSE ... KISS'N UP IS HARD TO DO!] *(sing melody)*

Part 4

It takes 2-Participants to bend down and stoop to the Up-Pa-dy Girls Club ... Kiss'n Up.

You see there's a Greater & Lesser love affair going on between "Ms. 6-figure" & Ms. 1-pay check away from being Broke."

There's 2-Agenda to be accomplished, one is to cover one's fears *(that her husband won't loose his job or leave her, or she loose hers too)* and the other just wants to practice the four-fingered hand wave of Ms. America.

Shopp'n hard, play'n Bridge, tea parties, dinners, and vacations at the Spa Ridge. Absent-minded, bittersweet, cordial dislikes, brownie points, and bulimic wanna-be's, try'n to carbon copy a role model of "shadow-ness." Snotty, Snooty, Superficial, and Moody. *This must be really hard to smooch your collagen lips* around this self-indulging, self-serving witch? But she's your best friend, and ya'll get your hair did together. Girrrl! can't you see that you're like fungus under her press-on fingernails. And your status makes her feel like a million bucks, your size "B" makes her size "A" feel like a double "D" cup. Ms. Pompous is bragg'n and constantly stabb'n, and you're trapped, jealous, and always lagg'n.

Sister, you've been a Vicious Victim, of Vocal Voodoo, actively hypnotizing you into a matrix of false hope, um hum! … no joke! Girl, know that your fate is to be great & wealthy and not rich and silicon healthy. So, follow the things that really matter.

Love, Peace, & Excellence are the Path. So laugh and take a bath in "Self-Worth."

[CAUSE … KISS'N UP IS HARD TO DO!] *(sing melody)*

♣ ♣ ♣ ♣ ♣ ♣ ♣ ♣ ♣ ♣ ♣ ♣

Poem:	*Kiss'n Up is Hard to Do!*
Inspiration:	*written on 08/17/05*
Annotations:	*I wrote this piece on an airplane to heading to Chicago for vacation. Yes, I was happy to be leaving my work place environment where I saw on a daily basis some form of Kiss'n up. I was extremely grateful for this vacation break!*
Dedications:	*To all the people in this world who have indulged in people-pleasing activities just because you thought it was the only way. I have news; this is not a healthy thing to put yourself through.*
Meditation:	*Exodus 20:3-5 "Thou shalt have no other gods before me. Thou shalt not make unto thee any graven image, or any likeness [of any thing] that [is] in heaven above, or that [is] in the earth beneath, or that [is] in the water under the earth: Thou shalt not bow down thyself to them, nor serve them: for I the Lord thy God [am] a jealous God, visiting the iniquity of the fathers upon the children unto the third and fourth [generation] of them that hate me;"*
Contemplations:	*Ask Yourself→ In your choices of friends and/or activities, is this what you really want for yourself?*
	Ask Yourself→ How proud of yourself are you?

Ask Yourself ➔ *What do you need in order to be all that you believe you've been created to be?*

Ask Yourself ➔ *Minus Family, Friends, and Co-workers, what have you done for yourself lately?*

IN ONES RIGHT MIND

In this day and age,
it is essential
to be in ones right mind,
at all times.
In other words,
in the unlikely event
that you happen to be
in the midst of
and in face of
people in a bad mood,
in a bad way,
in and of itself,
you may find yourself
in a pinch,
in cold-blood,
ready to say something
in poor taste.
In fact,
in front of,
and in spite of
who's watching,
you in the same breathe,
are in full swing,
and in retrospect
acting like the person
in a bad mood.
But you woke up
in seventh heaven,
in essence,
and in keeping with,

and in favor of
a person in a good mood.
So, in reality,
let toxic personalities
go in one ear
and out the other,
in a flash.
Because to stay in mint condition,
and in tune with life,
in a big way,
and in good spirits,
in real time,
and in a cold sweat,
we must resist
the small stuff
that puts us in a fix.
So, in the long run,
and in a nut shell,
and in hopes of
having a great day,
in no uncertain terms,
pray to be in the know,
and ...
In one's right mind at all time.

♣ ♣ ♣ ♣ ♣ ♣ ♣ ♣ ♣ ♣ ♣

Poem:	*In Ones Right Mind*
Inspiration:	*written on 11/03/05*
Annotations:	*I was inspired to write this because I witnessed that famous street commercial where one driver was violently honking at the car in front of him (yes, two men) and both got*

engaged in using their middle fingers to express themselves. And this was all because the 1st driver wouldn't run the red light.

Dedications: *To all the "Road-Rager's & "Stressed to the Max" people in this world.*

Meditation: <u>*Ephesians 4:26-27*</u> *"In your anger do not sin": Do not let the sun go down while you are still angry, and do not give the devil a foothold."*

Contemplations: *Ask Yourself*➜ *How well do you take care of your mental, physical, and spiritual self?*

Ask Yourself ➜ *What do you do to de-stress, rest, and rejuvenate yourself?*

Ask Yourself➜ *If you are raging, angry, out of your mind mad, ask yourself, what is this really about?*

DIVINE MATE

I refuse to choose him,
because ultimately I loose him.
I refuse to sell myself on a date,
eventually I become
Under the control of my mate.
I refuse to patch, plead, and live in
a fairy tale union.
Down the line my focus becomes
boredom, frustration, and a tolerated union.
You see, whether you're single, married, or
divorced two or three times,
your marriage to God should be your highest prize.
Intimacy with God is needed now,
and in the future too.
Without it,
your fulfillment will simply be a fraction of
what your Heavenly Father really desires for you.
Listen!
Just listen to the voice that whispers to you,
and laugh out loud from the blessings that tickle.
Remember, the covenant of gratitude is
the radio frequency of solitude.
So, Tune-in.
God's blessing and Love will always cover our foolish decisions.
But don't make choices that will devour your pure intentions.
Jesus says, my sheep know my voice,
and God's thoughts and ways are not like mine.
But if you spend time with your Divine,

your heart will know what's truth,
and the fruit of His vine.

Question: Are you the master of your own fate?
Or is your Divine mate the keeper of your gate?

♣ ♣ ♣ ♣ ♣ ♣ ♣ ♣ ♣ ♣ ♣ ♣

Poem:	*Divine Mate*
Inspiration:	*written on 06/09/02*
Annotations:	*My reflections of God (Christ) being my 1st love instead of other people and things.*
Dedications:	*The true Bride of Christ*
Meditation:	*Proverbs 16:3 "Commit thy works unto the Lord, and thy thoughts shall be established.*
	Ephesians 5:25-27 "husbands, love your wives, even as Christ also loved the church, and gave himself for it; That he might sanctify and cleanse it with the washing of water by the word, That he might present it to himself a glorious church, not having spot, or wrinkle, or any such thing; but that it should be holy and without blemish."
Contemplations:	*Ask Yourself → Who's your personal idol?*
	Ask Yourself → How do you view the word intimacy?
	Ask Yourself → How would you describe your intimacy with God?

LIVING IN REALITY

(*Sing Stanza*) Woke up this morning with my mind, stayed on Jesus....

But as soon as I pulled the covers from over my head,
my heart starts racing to the *pace* of this *place*
I live in called ...
"here & now."
As my eyes open to a blurry vision of this day,
I want to cling to keeping them shut....
but instead I ask myself, what will it bring?
Will I be able to meditate on its sweet melody?
Besides, I am breathing-warm,
in my right mind,
have the activities of my limbs, ...
I'm Super Woman, Right?!
Wrong.
Cause, my back hurts,
my legs-ache,
and I need some Tylenol cause
my thoughts-cry with all that needs to be done today.
Single mom,
with laundry, Cooking, Cleaning,
driving myself to work,
and "least-not forget,
the free taxi-cab service I provide for my children.
See the **Reality** of the situation is,
I'm tired before I even get started!
My virtuous girlfriend who lives in the land of Proverbs,
I need some of her contagious strength, ...
want to have lunch together some time,
but my calendar's always in "virtual Reality" mode

with my load & loads of stuff to do.
I'll have to get back with you
on us sipping tea
to how you maintain your strength and self-regard,
while gazing-hard into To-mor-rows Promise's singing …

***(Sing Stanza)* Woke up this morning with my mind, stayed on Jesus….**

See, in this "here & now,"
Reality requires my punctuality,
and in all practicality,
my unique personality to be
a dedicated person with individuality,
consecrated and set apart for sacred use.
But the Channel 9 News
is giving me the blues
with all the clue
on how to be "in this world" and of its politics.
Yes, I struggle to purify myself
from everything that contaminates my body and spirit
with being in the mix of it.
These closely knit hues of skin
try to seduce me with this noun called "division."
Divided we stand
to the collision course of
prejudice, hunger, injustice, and systematic inequities.
This thinking is like a Ecclesiastical Oxymoron;
not divine wisdom portrayed,
this is nothing but
religious political cognitive mental know-how.
A world who knows how to rub elbows,
create red-tape,

pollute the earth with fear,
hardened hearts, and boycott blame.
Shame on us,
because there's a massive log sticking out our brains
and we can't see.
And the reality is,
ignorance is *not* bliss
and me trying to be a part of the solution
and not the problem
is *no fun at all.*
I know my salvation
is linked to the abilities You gave me Lord,
to serve platters full of your Perfect Love.
But this Cat-eat-Mouse game
has my left-brain exhausted
and my right-brain defrosted
from heart-ache intonations of ...

(hum Stanza).... Woke up this morning with my mind stayed on Jesus.

See, Back to *Reality*,
and ... Back to the actualities of my spirituality....
and my abnormalities
in the duality of Yesterday's Future.
See this skin I "walk in"
is *Sutured* with the perception that everything's okay ...
But it's not,
and as my mind wonders astray....
I'm think'n out of my carnality and immorality
partially because
some "unknown person" cut me off on the road today.
So, now I'm pissed and stewing with revenge-type hate,

don't have a clue why.
But like chicken pox,
I realize my body is infected
with lots & lots of issues stuck in my heart-tissues....
there's fornication, divorce,
and adulterous thoughts.
And as the infection continues to show its blisters,
I see lying, cheating, violence, and disrespecting others.
Abuse, drug misuse,
bankruptcy, robbing Peter to pay Paul,
dodging phone calls from creditors,
my debt and greed,
lawsuits, lottery tickets, jackpots, tax collectors.
My late-to-work addiction,
anti-tithing affliction,
arrogance, arguments, betrayal,
AND boasting, greedy, gossip,
jealous, hypocritical judging,
profanity, rape,
self-deception, slander,
and the *misconception* that
falling into these temptations are okay,....
because all **you & I** need to do is
ask for forgiveness,
TO/MOR/ROW.
I'm venting with steam
to beam into the itchy-unclean
that this *Reality-Stuff* really brings.
I want to be washed
from any lifelong entanglements
of "the mundane"
or any "INSANE"

washing *your brain* as well as mine....
with "Deceptive Lies."
And my **Reality** is, ...
Lord ... please just,
needle and thread me with
YOUR TRUTH & WISDOM.
Because ...

(Sing Stanza) I woke up this morning with my Mind Stayed on Jesus.

♣ ♣ ♣ ♣ ♣ ♣ ♣ ♣ ♣ ♣ ♣ ♣

Poem:	*Living in Reality*
Inspiration:	*written on 11/12/06*
Annotations:	*Written for a comedy/poetry event at Colorado Christian Fellowship (my church home).*
Dedications:	*To all the down-to-earth, keep-it-real folks in the world that want some truth in the matter.*
Meditation:	*Isaiah 41:13* "For I the LORD thy God will hold thy right hand,
	saying unto thee, Fear not; I will help thee."
	2 Timothy 3:1-5 "This know also, that in the last days perilous times shall come. For men shall be lovers of their own selves, covetous, boasters, proud, blasphemers, disobedient to parents, unthankful, unholy, Without natural affection, trucebreakers, false accusers, incontinent, fierce, despisers of those that are good, Traitors, heady, highminded, lovers of pleasures more than lovers of God; Having a form of godliness, but denying the power thereof: from such turn away."*
Contemplations:	*Ask Yourself ➔ What's your reality like?*
	Ask Yourself ➔ Is your reality serving your well?

Ask Yourself ➔ *Do you see life as choice or circumstance?*

SHE'S JUST ANOTHER WOMAN

She has marble floors,
a housekeeper
and walnut doors.
the urban 4 by 4,
an Afro centric Name,
Gourmet meats,
and pedi-cured feet,
but now she has to take the heat
because her husband cheats.
(She's Just Another Woman!)

She's tall & talented,
Educated and degree-ed.
Smart but dumb.
Opening doors of opportunity to run … into false security.
She's numb.
She's a fashionable bum.
She's waddles around in cognac & rum.
Trapped by a man that controls,
he's crushed all her dreams and goals.
(She's Just Another Woman!)

She's plain-Jane.
without a focus or plan.
driving that mini-van.
High-school degree-ed,
not a scab on her knee,
She perfect-ly … alone.
Pop'n pills,
skinny down to the bone.

Dark circled eyes,
waiting by the phone,
waiting by the phone,
She's a puppet on his string,
Listening to a dial tone.
(She's Just Another Woman!)

She's Sunday-Only church girl,
with a white picket fence,
Bible collecting dust,
but a clean house is a must.
Keep'n Up…. tummy tucks, Bo-Tox,
and neighbors that compare notes.
Golf clubs, tea parties & fishing boats.
Just keep taking care of me & the children too.
I don't care how you treat me,
as long as the money keeps flowing through.
I just exist to fulfill the American Dream,
I'm not really on your team
What do you mean,
We're not close,
we just live to boast,
& make sure we have the most.
Just bring home the bacon & I'll fry it up in a pan.
Because tomorrow I'll be working on my tan.
(She's Just Another Woman!)

She's Fuss'in & Cuss'in,
Laugh'n & Crack'n,
Cook'n & Shopp'n,
Working 2 Jobs,
yes, She's always Hopp'n.
Ms. Multi-tasker, tired from an unbalanced life.

She's always had to fight.

Fight'n to wake-up.

Fight'n to find rest.

Fight'n to stay alive.

Fight'n to make a little ... best.

Fight'n to find Self-worth.

Survival <u>is</u> of the fittest.

Nice Girls finish last, but Bad Girls just Finish.

Left alone to figure it out.

Her mind is full of Hurt & Doubt.

She's Super-"WORN-OUT"—Women.

Her father left her & husband too.

SO—WHAT'S NEW?

(She's Just Another Woman!)

She's the Rugged Old-Navy Type.

Thinks nurturing children is a bunch of hype.

Just give her some Sperm in a tube.

Instead of Jiffy-Bread,

It's Jiffy Lube.

Dirty Nails,

She's Butcher-Block Sandy.

She's wants to kill the man that stole her little-girl candy.

Rambo Virgin, ready to cut every man's throat.

Ready to sink his boat.

Just Note.

She can only taste the lips of her female other.

Remembering her Rapist was her Uncle & Step-Brother.

(She's Just Another Woman!)

She wears High Heels ... Spiked, Pointed & Red.

She's try'n to get off that High-Horse,

And out of her Brass Canopy Bed.

Can't seem to roll-out ... cause she's <u>high</u>.

High! ... in those high-heels.

Feeling Tall in her Delusional-Head.

Spinning and running from Fear & Pain.

The pain of the daddy she'll never Gain.

Feeling numb is her desire sun-up to sun-down.

You know they say, "Girls Just want to have Fun!"

She's try'n to find safety in the drug called "genocide."

She want to ride to the other side,

because her high has come down and died.

Now the strut becomes a slow-focused-walk.

She can't talk, ... & she's lost,

in her own world of dead.

She clicks her heels 3 times,

back to that brass canopy bed.

(She's Just Another Woman!)

<u>Part II</u>—Hey Woman!, Hey Girl! My Sister & Friend.

Put behind you those valley-dark-days.

Believe me, It's Only a Phase.

I've had a taste of your reality ... you see,

But there's only one way to be all that you've been purposed to Be.

Just Wash yourself Off

And Begin, My Friend.

Begin to turn from the past,

and never look back.

Jesus will usher you in to a new life without Lack.

Hey Woman!, Hey Girl! My Sister & Friend.

Your perfume is fragrant and come from the Father above.

From the Pit to the Palace,

Is where you'll find HIS LOVE.

He will cover His EVE,

with all that you need.

Just know, God is your Lead.

Hey Woman!, Hey Girl! My Sister & Friend.

He will meet you when you've decided to exit the Pit.

So don't quit!

Just Press & Fight,

and never loose Sight of the Light.

Because you're no longer "Just Another Women."

But You are.... *His-Beloved!*

♣ ♣ ♣ ♣ ♣ ♣ ♣ ♣ ♣ ♣ ♣ ♣

Poem:	*She's Just Another Woman*
Inspiration:	*written on 03/31/04*
Annotations:	*I saw little pieces of me in each women described but I unlearned what I needed to and learned some truth about myself as beautiful woman of God.*
Dedications:	*Deceived American Women*
Meditation:	*Luke 4:18* "*Preach Deliverance to the Captive.*
	Jeremiah 31:3 "*the LORD hath appeared of old unto me, saying, Yea, I have loved thee with an everlasting love: therefore with lovingkindness have I drawn thee.*"
Contemplations:	*Ask Yourself* → *What's deceiving you?*
	Ask Yourself → *Are you asleep in your life or fully awake?*
	Ask Yourself → *Gauge your self-worth for 1 to 10.*

TORN BETWEEN 2 SONGS

(Sing melody) He (meaning the old boyfriend) *was Strum'n my pain with his fingers, Sing'n my life with his words....*

It's killing me softly to
feel this songs play my inner ear
with sweet elliptical interactions
laced in the afterglow of
exhaling breathless breaths,
and hoops of love that echo from my womb.
I glance left at my "ring-less" finger
to find myself staring at ceilings,
and hear deep snoring from
the someone who
thought he went to heaven and back,
but only experienced adrenaline
at the free-throw line of false promises.

See, it's a mind game,
and the aftermath,
minus the afterglow,
makes tears flow from my heart
as I kick these sheets off
to ask for forgiveness
laced in starting over
after waiting 6-long-years.
And I remember
He rested on the 7th day,
knowing a new day would begin.
See baby today,
I want you to know
there's more to these virgin hips,

my pomegranate-stained lips,
and that every drip of innocence
that laced my thighs with your,
is MY CRY that....
this time,
I will not partake
in Seductions Fruit.

You whisper,
what's on my mind,
so let me introduce you to
reproductions monthly fights
of coffee pot peculations
and this brown sugar's cream,
my estrogen wet dreams ...
I mean,
I feel like,
I've been cursed with the experience,
yet blessed with loveable rips of reason,
beyond the logical
of its mountaintop euphoria.
You can't be anything else
other than divine intervention
prescribed for handcuffed connections
that only my delicate wrist could bare.
Yes, I fight "TO NOT"
cloud my thoughts with imaginations ...
of "US."
Because you see....
I'm Torn between 2 songs,
Two worlds,
Two Kisses,

Two Whispers,
Two embraces, ...

(Sing melody) He (meaning the old boyfriend) *was Strum'n my
    pain with his fingers, Sing'n my life with his words....*

And your words
are sweet aromas
that breath LOVE
and I desire your Ora
to surround my thermal Zones
with electricity minus the shock.
See, I want everlasting
HIGH VOTAGE in this 3-prong plug.
Nothing but the Trinity experience
beyond the fork in the road,
not some short-lived love.
See we can't reminisce on those
Discovery-type knobs you
pushed, pulled, licked, tasted,
in order to know my *primal nature;*
"FELINE."
And that "chorus line" we both screamed,
in the midst of the storm,
IT'S NOT ENOUGH!
Because you see,
there is another,
the one we moaned,
He's sing'n to my deep places,
minus the sex,
the ring,
the house,

and all those wonderful things that you bring.

Sweetie, it's you, me, and our maker,
Not you, me and some heart breaking moment.
And ever time I imagine
those thick interludes of hearts thumping
to gasp for air,
declaring epiphany's oneness,
I bring blood to my bottom lip,
to erase me back.
Then, I ask myself,
Who's really on 1st?
I guess, it depends on
this mama's overall thirst of the situation.
So, (dammit!) *somebody!* ... give me a glass of water....
cause I'm willing to loose you,
so you can choose what's right.

Yes, my "head voice" says,
drink of your delicious libations.
But the "Strong-quiet Voice" says ...
there's one true promise, if I wait.
See, I'm willing to free-fall to all of this,
And DAMN!,
it's so hard
to not put you on a pedestal
equal to our maker,
because honey
you served me like a happy Hebrew Slave,
reaching freedoms promised land.
And by the way,
your name reads in the sand,....

"Black King."

See, I know your family jewels
were designed to rest between your perfect help-mate,
so Eyes-closed,
I swipe my head against this wine glass,
and I Ask,
"who can fulfill OUR real thirst?"
See Baby,
I'm so hungry in my soul
for comfort beyond food or touch,
I take every fingernail
to let go of this grip,
cause I don't want my love canal
to ache with yearning for you.
See, I'm torn between 2 songs,
Two worlds,
Two Kisses,
Two Whispers,
Two Embraces,
Two Promises.

Cause He is now (meaning: Jesus ... as my 1st Love) *... Strum'n my
pain with His fingers ... Sing'n my life with His words ...*

Poem:	*Torn between 2 Songs*
Inspiration:	*written on 01/14/07*
Annotations:	*Conquering temptations in the mist of the storm, ... no, I mean thunderstorm, ... no hurricane,.... no tsunami, ...*

no typhoon. Hell all of it bundled together; it's a hellified temptation!

Dedications:

Single Women who are pressing to wait for "The Promise" and not settling for fairy tale wish.

Meditation:

<u>Matthew 6:13</u> "And lead us not into temptation, but deliver us from evil: For thine is the kingdom, and the power, and the glory, for ever. Amen."

<u>1 Samuel 15:22</u> "And Samuel said, Has Jehovah delight in burnt-offerings and sacrifices, As in hearkening to the voice of Jehovah? Behold, obedience is better than sacrifice, Attention than the fat of rams.

Contemplations:

Ask Yourself → What tools do you have to help you make good choices for yourself?

Ask Yourself → How well do you listen to your inner voice (the Holy Spirit) or what some term as your gut, or intuition?

Ask Yourself → What parts of your life have been by design and parts have not?

LETTER TO A BROTHA WHO'S A M.D.

Dear Doctor … Look Good, Feel Good, & Taste Good too!
I'm feel'n poetic,
So let me recite some Black Shakespeare to you,
It's my anti-apologetic and general anesthetic.
Cause Hell Yeh, I'm sick! … of you!,
So get ready for some "me Nurse" & "you Doctor" kind of truth.

(pause)

"To be Chased" or "Not be Chased!"
That is the question I face with you,
on who's *gonna win* this mental race called,
You better respect the way you handle My BODY, cause it's Priceless!

I'm so sick and tired of treading water in "this Love Game." … with
     you.
See, there's a fine-line between "Stalking me" and "Chasing me."
Cause your stalk'n ain't nothing but.…
hot pursuits of YOU cool'n places between your pants, nose, teeth, &
     toes,
all because of your wet-laced imaginations of what I *feel like* minus
     my cloths.
Track'n my pheromone-trails like a dog-in-heat,
And.… when I've said "yes," to your speed racer,
Just know that, "the glove", "the pills", and IUD,
Is a clear guarantee that I'm not the one.… to take home to.… *yo
     Mommie,*
Nor am I interested in panting hard labor to bear children *for thee.*

Yes, your medical degree has allowed you to be,
a Man toy, Play boy, Gigolo, and Sweet talk'n Corporate thug,
and you've stalked all kinds of "alley cat hoes,"

making her sing for her supper.

But don't—make the mistake of hitt'n me with your player's card,

Cause baby, I'm tempted to play you like the "quack" that your are,

Pretending to love me,

When all you wanted was practice **with yo** Forceps and Stethoscope.

And…. after seeing that the price was right,

I suggest you cancel all appointments,

And smell THIS "Black Coffee" tonight.

Hell yeah, I hope your taking a sip,

And…. I promise not to poison you…. with anything but flashbacks
   of "show ya right."

See, I know your game,

she does everything she can to,

catch your eyes, AND <u>balls</u>, and how well your wallet <u>falls</u> into her lap,

but she's acting like a <u>drone</u>, and lost herself to foreplay's <u>moan</u>.

But you See, I'm "Ol Skool," … and came along when Black & White
   TV's were hot. So I'm not putt'n up with yo crap!

See, "This Sistah" was brought up to be Courted & not Stalked …
   Mister Big Stuff! *(sing melody)* Who do you think you are?, Mister
   Big Stuff! You never gonna get my love!

Cause I want to talk about what happened to that Dog chase-the-Cat
   type love?

Panting after me with your tongue-twirling taster happily waiting,

As—-long—-as—-I—-say—-so, … *Negro!*

Yes, I AM *that kind of girl* … whose familiar with every grove in your
   tongue,

& how breathing activities happen in your lungs,

Yes, you suppose to be "Sprung" … over me,

Not me over you.

See, them alley cat hoes ain't gotta clue.

A gentleman that knows how "to chase,"…. & targets my neck bone,

& his Eyes gaze into the *very deep* parts of my <u>soul</u>,

With the <u>goal</u> of respecting my body like a Queen.

Hell Yeh, I'm the queen of my THRONE.

See, I look around and I'm blown away by what I see now days,

Alley cat hoes don't know when to stop play'n games,

Besides the cereal box says Tricks are for kids.

So what I'm try'n to convey is,

This Feline needs to be chased, ... And that's the way it is!

SO stop wasting your folded arms on who's gonna make the next move,

Hell, What you try' to prove?, Who the FELINE.... me or you?

And another thing,....

This is my last letter to you, ... so take it like a man,

Cause I ... sho'll ain't gonna argue ... with-yo ...
    "white-coat-wearing" self,

cuz you really should be wearing what you are ... SCRUBS!

See Mr. M.D., *let me tell you something* ...

if I ain't a subliminal thought that pops in your head minus any
    physical stimulation,

Then here's my verbal combination of "Hell" to the "No,"

Yes, You gotta flow out of my life, meaning you gotta go!

See Brotha, my love goes deeper than how Niagara falls ... from my
    sugar walls,

Or *how well* my Intellect recalls,....

my good genes & pretty face,

this *big butt* and *little waist.*

See, if you fail to respect *this* "Lin-guis-tic" Queen,

By all means, you bests believe,

I'm hold'n sick leave down all by myself.

And my self-affirmations are "prophetic re-births" of who God says I
    am.

So I'll be Dammed!, ...
if I'm stalked like an alley cat hoe.

So Brotha, at the next "Dog Show," ... If you want to reach new
    plateau's,
1ˢᵗ of all, don't look in my direction,
Cause this is my affectionate "love letter" of correction to you,
And Yes, I AM ... rejecting you,
   ... **Cause YOU FAILED to** *"Respectfully"*.... **Chase the Cat!**

♣ ♣ ♣ ♣ ♣ ♣ ♣ ♣ ♣ ♣ ♣

Poem:	*Letter to a Brotha who's a M.D.*
Inspiration:	*written on 03/29/07*
Annotations:	*Yeah, had to close a chapter in my life, so a new story would play in my mind, one where I'm in the driver's seat ... and Christ as my navigator.*
Dedications:	*To Karen Thompson, Denita Sconiers, and Janemarie Newton who are my very good friends. I thank you because I was able to be transparent without you being judgmental. You helped me to pinpoint this issue that I needed to write about.*
Meditation:	*Matthew 5:28 "But I say unto you, that whosoever looketh on a woman to lust after her hath committed adultery with her already in his heart."*
Contemplations:	*Ask Yourself* → What mental stories do you have in your mind that hold you back from moving forward in your life?
	Ask Yourself → How do you communicate your choices?
	Ask Yourself → What is on decision you can act upon to help you move forward?

BOUNDARIES
UNVEILED

Boundaries Unveiled
are my
personal limits
Inhaled.
Okay, you *Digging* me?

I SAID, NO!

No!
Listen, I said ... "Noe-wah!" ...
and *pleeze*, just "Go-wah!"
Do I need to say Naw!, ...
in fact, Heck-Naw!
Oh yeah, I'm raw!....
and I will be expressing myself ... y'all.
Oh, you don't understand!....
read my lips ...
"nnN" "ooO".... Bro!
Okay, I'll be polite!
No Thank You Sis!
and here's my floating Kiss....
So, Let's review,
No Thank You Boo.

No, is Okay ... Today.
No, is Protection that gives me Direction.
No, is Choice and my Head-Voice.
No, is my Boundary Fence
Yes, my Defense to false Pretense.

I—Said—No!
My "Yes" Lessons have taught me
the "No" Answer ... and
My "No" Lessons have kept me
from "Drama's Cancer."
For the sake of Self-Love
is a good reason for "NO."
For the sake of Heavenly Love
is a good reason all the time.

He's protecting me from
Grime, Slime, and Victimless Crime.

Why handle life so frivolously weak?
Meek wavering Yes's Shriek ...
Unflavoring Grey Yes's,
And Thoughtless Yes's ...
lead to "Explosive" No's.
Corrosive Verbal Blows,
and rows and rows of
uncertainty is exposed, I suppose.

Just Say No!

The Attraction of Distractions,
And Drama with endless Commas,
Just plain-Old dumb Stuff,
Enough of the rough fluff, stubb'n your Big Toe,
Heck, Just Say, "No!"

Poem:	*I said, No!*
Inspiration:	*written on 03/30/01*
Annotations:	*Setting Boundaries*
Dedications:	*To all the people that think that saying "No" is a bad, con-victing, selfish thing. It's not.*
Meditation:	*I Corinthian 13:12 "For now we see through a glass, darkly; but then face to face: now I know in part; but then shall I know even as also I am known."*
Contemplations:	*Ask Yourself* → What's the mid-point between yes and no?

Ask Yourself ➔ What personal boundaries have you set for yourself?

Ask Yourself ➔ What support do you need to say No?

No Test Drives Allowed

Back in the day,
my daddy taught me to drive.
Open parking lots,
wide range distances between
telephone poles and stop signs.
His strong voice,
don't burn the clutch,
just ease up,
and not too much.

But the day I past the test,
license in hand,
I let my hair down
to a new experience.
Scarf flowing in the humidity,
music thump'n
like the heart beat of an elephant.

I was free to roam the streets,
scanning panoramic views
of chocolate city's Hoop-laced parks,
barbeque smoke,
corner peddlers
selling me peanuts in a bag
and gold chains
all before the red light changed.

Yes, I was free
to drive my own world,
in my rusty old Toyota,

the leftover car,
a priceless gem,
my 4 wheels,
with no fancy rims.

But Suddenly,
something changed without my daddy in the car,
Now, I hear whistling and see thumbs-up
from flirtatious hick-hikers,
verbal city-chat,
and the noisy flavors of
South-Side Chicago,
the hood I know from head to toe.

Catching me off-guard as a new driver,
I get extra attentions from
the testosterone-occupied male species
and the heavy raps
from all 21 flavors of brothers,
no ice cream truck in site,
but I see "vanilla swirl"
to "hot fudge chocolate mocha delight,"
.... Lord have mercy!,
help me!,
cause I'm in.... a new kind of street-life fight.

Now, I don't remember this
being in the driver's Ed Test.
I thought defensive driving was
to avoid insurance claims,
not candy cane moments
entertaining me with "sales campaigns,"

causing me mental stains,
heartaches, and sweaty armpits.

Brotha, can you get a little more original
in your bold
high-pitched dramatic lip licking,
implying with your subtle innuendo's
that I'm the only one you said that line to today.
Now, I respect your desire
to acknowledge beauty when you see it,
but let me skool you,
my mama didn't raise no fools.

Then the brother says ...
Can I get those digits? *No*
Girl, you know you fine! *Thanks You*
Do fries come with that shake? *No*
Your man must be stupid to leave you alone! *Really*
Can I ride in your car? *I don't think so!*

Now Listen Breaux,
I need you to pay attention
and hang on to my every word blow-by-blow.
You see, I'm not swinging my hair,
or biting my lips,
batt'n my eyes,
or sway'n my hips.
My smile is not a suggesting tease
and I'm not raising my eyebrows
to say I'm easy.
Trust me,
this ain't planet of the Ape-girls.

And I'm not playing these games
of subliminal mind-wars.

You see, I'm wearing the latest fashion
and starting a new trend.
<u>***Check it out.***</u>
This trend is a treasure
that will not be a desperate measure
of how much pleasure your ego can forgo.
See, this is untouchable,
unswayed,
untasted,
unmoved
by your telepathic affirmations
that I'm delicious to look at.
Besides, <u>like a</u> "one-arm push-up,"
you need to back off....
because between my momma and her drama
threatening me to not get myself in trouble
and my daddy shoot'n you with his double barrel shot gun,
I don't think we'll be sing'n that song
"Always and Forever."

When my hormones are raging out of control
paging your mind with pheromones
engaging you in a unique perfume
un-identifiable by the same sex,
you need to recognize,
but keep walk'n
cause "No test drives are allowed!"....
Wake-up and smell the coffee
and not the waves of scent

that captivated your lack of self-control,
lucid subconscious
and storehouse of amplified imagination.

You see, in *this bosom,*
my heart-muscle has an inward affection
for the Man of all men,
the Daddy of all daddy's,
and the testosterone of all hormones.
Yes, He sits on a throne,
and mounts my settings with
diamonds laced in 18 Karat gold.
What were you thinking;
this ain't no "cubic zirconium!"
These gems,
this life-giving canal,
will be untouched
by what you clutch with your fist ...
a little bit too much!

The flirt.
The tease.
The Urge.
The Itch.
Reminds me of,
The Crabs,
the Herpes,
V.D.,
and AIDS.
Boy or Boy
what bewitching gifts
you're willing to trade.

<u>The Itch.</u>
<u>The Urge.</u>
<u>The Tease.</u>
<u>The Flirt.</u>
Reminds me that
this skirt
will abstain
from the rain of insane thoughts
washing my left-brain with logic
and my right brain with
random perverted intuition.

I know God made you
as an <u>individual</u> who is very visual,
but the heavens have made me
a virgin,
chase,
innocent,
full of virtue,
and grace,
intensely saturated with pureness,
undiluted with cravings,
and unmixed by provoking words ...
because baby ...
I'm saving it!

Now brother,
I know your hommies
are looking this way,
and it appears like this conversation
has gone in your favor,

so as a face-savor,
I'll give you a hug for free,
and I remind you that
my daddy said ...
"No Test Drives Allowed in my Car!"

Poem:	*No Test Drives Allowed*
Inspiration:	*written on 05/03/06*
Annotations:	*Self-Pride, Abstaining, being a teenager & human.*
Dedications:	*To my Daddy & my teen daughters.*
Meditation:	*Psalms 139:14 "I will praise thee; for I am fearfully and wonderfully made: marvelous are thy works; and that my soul knoweth right well."*
Contemplations:	*Ask Yourself → Who is your greatest champion (Advocate, Cheerleader, Motivator) in your life?*
	Ask Yourself → What standards do you have for yourself?
	Ask Yourself → When is it okay for you to be numero uno (1st)?

COME OUT YOUR CRAZY COCOON!

Lunatic!,
Disturbed!,
Ignoramus!,
Idiot!,
You Brain-sick!,
Wacky Ass!,
Bizarre!,
Maniac!.
Now, these are all the words I can think of,
That describe people.... Who ...
were born normal,
But act like a butt naked fool!
Yes, I have some, ... in my family.
And See, I ain't gonna argue with you,
cause I'll be wasting my time,
But I love you so,
I'm gonna spit some truth
from this tongue,
And hopefully it will reach
your Psycho mind.
Do you realize that
you're enwrapped in your own crap
of nonsense,
making no-pretense,
& always on the defense about
why nobody calls you
or offers to pick you up.
You need to come out your crazy cocoon!,
All shriveled-up like a prune,
frowning, rolling your eyes,

mumbling every profanity under your breath,

speaking death into your situation.

And when you start doing that "woe is me" ... speech.

There's a big glow called

"misery loves company"

and trust me,

you start petitioning my migraines

to start their engines.

Yeah, nothing but Rotten words

coming out of your mouth,

your heart is full of doubt,

complaining, gossiping,

acting like a space-cadet,

sweating people just because they're smiling,

making my stomach upset

with your guilt-laden,

depressing conversations.

YOU NEED TO COME OUT YOUR CRAZY COCOON!

Everybody else is afraid to tell you,

but not Ol Skool!

This is like Sci-fi, Extrasensory, & Weird!

You're not being creative and eccentric.

I can appreciate the authentic

multi-dimensional language of

Poetry-in-motion when I see it.

This is an unpolished notion called "Tragic,"

as if by magic,

you can out your mama's womb this way.

I don't thing so!

You know who you are,

and I'll be check'n in on you from time to time,

to see if the new moon

has moved your hibernation of "Cocoon"
to some form of "Caterpillar transformation."
And to my dismay....
I'm reminded everyday....
that you an I have the same mama & daddy.
So right now, I have a headache,
and I can't stay,
So somebody please give me some Tylenol,
so I can seriously pray!

Poem:	*Come out your Crazy Cocoon*
Inspiration:	*written on 05/15/06*
Annotations:	*It is good to encourage one another!.... and some people need raw encouragement.*
Dedications:	*To people having a moment ... you know who you are!*
Meditation:	*Proverbs 29:11 "A fool uttereth all his mind: but a wise man keepeth it in till afterwards."*
Contemplations:	*Ask Yourself → Who is this mess really about?*
	Ask Yourself → Will you stop to listen to the messenger?
	Ask Yourself → Do you value truth? even when it hurts?

YEAH, WE BE LOUD!

Sitt'n on my back patio,
I could hear the neighbors,
4 doors down,
laughing, crack'n,
hollering to the beat of
black-folk adult conversations.
Did you ever wonder why, we be so loud?

Now, let's not cloud the cerebral
with your ignorant rude song of judgment.
I see that little white Thought-Cloud
pop above your head
and it reads …
Oh my God!, they-are-so-Noisy!
and why are they yelling at each other?!!!
No, my uneducated sister & brother,
instead,
let me skool you on
how we actually love each other.

You see,
this enjoyment is like
"passionate-emotion"
bottled-up with happiness & friendship
just because
we carry the same hue of freeness
conveyed as
sharing truth with the someone,
whom I can relate.
So, my message is,

don't hate,
my neighborly backyard roommates.
Your hatred is nothing but
a state of being bleached in
"Sa-dity-fied-ness"
as you look over your white picket fence
full of splinters, termites,
and lead-based paint,
as you smile & wave,
I see the complaint is still all over your face.

Get ready,
cause here comes another blasting uproar
of rhetoric, empty-talk, and empty-air.
See, let me skool you on
our unique expressive style.
It's an aphrodisiac to
stimulate the core
to speak funny-sexy-words
that need to be heard.
The art of finishing sentences
is the genius IQ of infinity
connected to how we
touch basis with
bringing together
the celebration of
a dialect called "deliciously-loud"
with bellows of endless laughter!

So, don't try to hush us up,
because the rush with only have me
pump-up the volume's magnitude,

to a level where you either hate it,
or want to join in on this
closely knit group
of being "ear-splitting brass cymbals."
HELL YEAH, WE BE LOUD!
Nodding to the bob of those
lightening rod moments,
men against women & vice versa,
conversing about the female perspective
and the male view-point;
the paradigm's chime of
big-time opinions,
teaming-up to have articulations
of one voiceless voice.

Bellyaching & shak'n with laughter,
glances of agreement,
listening for the opportunity to
blast into a space that allows my
interjection of agreement.
Yes, I know what you mean!
Boldness expressed as high-fives,
rolling eyes,
and hugs that glare with.... I truly Care!
You know what I mean?
Daring to be corny & funny,
Daring to walk in the footsteps of
"Comic-Views" amusing jokes,
and "def Poetry's" spoken word folks.
Yeah, we entertain each other with
smiles on faces,
and vocals that have the audacity to be

unexplainable,
don't make sense,
yet have immense amounts of
intense flashbacks
that lace the rooms atmosphere.
Oh! No you didn't! ...
Blatant slapstick's of flashy rudeness,
and explosive songs singing....
"You know you ain't right,"
so let's fight in this verbal boxing ring,
"ding-ding",
and figure-out how to
out-talk,
out-laugh,
and gasp in the freedom of
laughing-out candidly,
the free-spoken,
out-spoken words,
of artful loudness in us ...
that will never cease to exist! ...
so don't be pissed!!!!

But in case you're that neighbor
who will always stay pissed,
let me assist you with
taking the wooden log
out your posterior
before you call 911
concerning the splinter in my baby finger.
Just take your cheesy,
lack of wisdom calling,
judgmental,

no good,
disapproving self,
back to the couch
that grip your butt-cheeks with
the Lamaze method of....
as you breath
to be displeased,
irritated, pissed, peeved,
concerning your opinion
about how you rate me.
My final text message is
"You can kiss where the sun don't shine" ...
which means,
if you want to stay in your own world of prejudgment,
that's with me ...
I skooled you nicely,

So like it or not....
THAT'S WHY.... WE BE LOUD!

♣ ♣ ♣ ♣ ♣ ♣ ♣ ♣ ♣ ♣ ♣ ♣

Poem:	*Yeah, We be Loud!*
Inspiration:	*written on 05/29/06*
Annotations:	*Don't Judge what you don't know. Ignorance will always keep you in your own world of darkness.*
Dedications:	*To my not so friendly neighbors with a different skin color than me.*
Meditation:	*Matthew 7:1-5 "Judge not, that ye be not judged. For with what judgment ye judge, ye shall be judged: and with what measure ye mete, it shall be measured to you again. And why beholdest thou the mote that is in thy brother's eye, but*

considerest not the beam that is in thine own eye? Or how wilt thou say to thy brother, Let me pull out the mote out of thine eye; and, behold, a beam is in thine own eye? Thou hypocrite, first cast out the beam out of thine own eye; and then shalt thou see clearly to cast out the mote out of thy brother's eye."

Contemplations: *Ask Yourself* ➔ *Do you see people as creative, resourceful, and human regardless of their ethnicity? Why or Why not?*

Ask Yourself ➔ *What zaps you of your time and energy?*

Ask Yourself ➔ *Are you aware that your perspective may be limiting you?*

STANDING
IN MY SIZE 6
STILETTO'S

Planting My Feet in Size 6 Stiletto's
Is all about Learning Me,
Loving Me,
and
Being Me,
you see!

SOLITUDE IN MOTION

Peaceful strokes of God's breath
divide the strands of my hair.
As I Inhale Love, I Exhale life's Impurities.
It's Peaceful.
As I sit still on the sands by the Ocean,
watching a crab crawl out of its shell.
Every ... Subliminal ... Detail,
I see,
in slow motion.
I receive Wisdom's Message,
in a blink of an eye.
The rays of light penetrate my heart with truth.
My Queen-ness landscapes a scene,
shining forth like serene sweet 16.
Greatness within see's *all*,
ready to bring to my recall
all that is there for me.
Waves of Love flow ... Into-Me-You-See,
Palm Trees, fresh air, & New Beginnings are at my reach.
I reach out & Touch & Fly like the birds.
My wings reflect the color of the Sky
and my Heart is as pure as the Ocean water.
I frequently return, because.... Solitude Quenches my Thirst.

Poem:	*Solitude in Motion*
Inspiration:	*written during the month of 04/2002*
Annotations:	*Solitude in your soul is a priceless commodity*

Dedications:	*To My Lord, Savior, and Maker.*
Meditation:	*Job 22:21 "Acquaint now thyself with him, and be at peace: thereby good shall come unto thee."*
	Psalms 4:8 "I will both lay me down in peace, and sleep: for thou, LORD, only makest me dwell in safety."
	Psalms 37:11 "But the meek shall inherit the earth; and shall delight themselves in the abundance of peace."
	Psalms 37:37 "Mark the perfect man, and behold the upright: for the end of that man is peace."
Contemplations:	*Ask Yourself → What's wonderful in your life right now?*
	Ask Yourself → What's missing?
	Ask Yourself → When do you make room for quiet time for you?

CROSS-SECTIONS OF A WOMAN

Today, my cross-section-silhouette reads
Young-hearted,
Experienced,
Diva!
Divinely divided by
equal parts of
"remarkable,"
"valuable,"
and "Delightful."
Deliciously digg'n every thing about myself,
because you see
my greatness was decided by
Heavenly prescribed thinking,
I am a Prophesy
from Wisdom's truth-giving tongue,
THE KISS made manifest.

But you see,
I didn't know THE TRUTH about me
for a long time.
I had to go thru the boot camps of life,
dressing down,
cramping my style,
in hard hats and steel-toe boots,
just to survive drama's dark holes.

But epiphany moments taught me to
conquer naive,
master being really mean, ...
Hate the notion of the word "Average",
to a girl who clawed her way

to find her "true self."
Digg'n my fingernails
in the Perfume Called "Estrogen,"
finding the main-vein's tenacity
to leave generations of
that unconditional-type Love.

See, life's distractions
tried to trip me up ...
but on the horizontal,
side and aerial view....
I met a lady enriched in
high-pitched enunciations of saying
"I am," ...
the perfect scent of pheromones
yours nose can't smell,
but only "wise men"
and other "Diva's" can identify.

Woman, step into your panties and bra's,
get rid of your Vigilantes and Scars....
"toss out" those dingy bloomer and mediocre-type Bra's too.
Women get bold,
buy yourself some Lace & Satin,
love yourself,
herself,
myself,
oneself,
ourselves.
Find yourself sistah!
Take pride in you,
and most of all....
prove yourself to yourself.

See, the "real she" is
a "chess piece"
designed to have a population profile of
check-mate,
no games,
she's simply "anti-brut,"
the "female-aristocrat,"
the "authentic-fairy,"
who's uterus, breast, & ovaries
interpret the word PMS.
Yeah, you need to roll with it,
lean with it,
and deal with it! ...
as her internal tambourines harmonize
to the beat of shedding tears
for the "*potential*" for new life.
Sway to her mood *swings*
like Bob Marley sings "No woman, No Cry."
As a matter fact,
he forgot to say, "No woman, No Child!"
Nations are birthed from your labor pains,
Girl, Do you realize who we are!!!?

See.... I am,
music-in-motion,
my walk,
the sway of my hips
are the Lyrics,
and my bounce
sets the tempo to all the music
God allowed to be created.

Listen Sisters,
just extend yourself to the heavenly rim,
where the cloud-maker
downloads features of character for you,
teach'n you how to
trade & export your Milk & Honey
and not give it away for free.
Tap-in & capture
the essence of the female "Prima Donna" that you are.
Your tears,
your prayers,
your tenacity,
your strength to fight
without breaking your fingernails
is the inward Spirit that rest between your bosom.

Yes, her biographical outline speaks!
Her profile is lovely, majestic and soft.
She is Virtue's life story.
This *is* a cross section of a women.
And Like I said!...., I'm a young-hearted, experienced, Diva.

So, What's your Cross-section, Sistah?

Poem:	*Cross-Sections of a Woman*
Inspiration:	*written on 07/06/06*
Annotations:	*I was thinking about "Self-Worth" from the (estrogen-occupied-female species) woman's.... perspective.*
Dedications:	*To every female, young, old, and unborn. So, read this to my (& your) granddaughters too.*

Meditation: <u>*Philippians 3:14*</u> *"I press toward the mark for the prize of the high calling of God in Christ Jesus."*
<u>*2 Corinthians 7:16*</u> *"I rejoice therefore that I have confidence in you in all things."*

Contemplations: *Ask Yourself* → *As a woman, what are you proud of about yourself?*

Ask Yourself → *As a woman, how much "Me Time" do you take per week?*

Ask Yourself → *As a woman, what gets in the way of your "Me Time?"*

RED KOOL-AID

See, my Sister (Staci) and I,
we should have never froze that
Red Kool-Aid in a paper Dixie Cup.
Our homemade Popsicle,
no wooden stick,
just licks & licks
from the tip of my tongue
to my pomegranate-stained lips.
Now, I'm all grown-up
and ingrain**ed** forever
with "this juice" pumping through my veins,
the Red-dye has
wonderfully messed-up my brain,
see it's raining lady bugs,
chili peppers and champagne,
cause I'm celebrating the fact that
"You Don't Know Me!"

Kool-Aid,
all in the grooves of my tongue,
staining my throat to my lungs,
reaching my cerebral with earthquakes,
making heart-aches of Self-talk.
Fear not Tami, for I am with you ...
The Red Kool-Aid has infected your body
with "ALL" the fire of your desire.

Hey, you want to know....
What color are my eyes?
Blood Shot Cherry.
What Flow'n in these veins?

A Flamed birthed by a virgin Named Mary.
AND How does this shell Salsa Dance?
Like Crimson Red Rivers of Boldness carrying all of Truths Coldness!
SEE! … You don't know me!

I hope you see Fire in my Tongue.
See, I might teach you the Word,
Pray with you,
give you two pecks on your cheeks,
to encourage you.
Ain't no Red-Tape,
I just cut to the chase,….
nicely,
try'n to *transfix*
"Dark Red" *antics* of reprimands
and common sense.

My RED-stained tongue has taken over.
Yes, I am the Whipper-Snapper
from here and now.
Slow to speak
and quick to wiretap in on
listening sessions of confession,
short-lived depressions
or mountain-top progressions.
See, you can't Clap-on or Clap-me-off,
I AM Unstoppable with righteous rhymes,
for *this* lifetime.

See you *(meaning Satan)* tried to PIMP me
with your *Cherry-Pick'n Bible-Bashing,*
"Low Hang'n Fruit Self."
Who you try'n to Pimp?
You can't make "pimp juice" out of Red!

See I was 50 steps ahead of your evil foolishness.
"The Experience" just made some permanent stains
under my skin,
so now,
I'm just grounded in being
Red Hot Tamales on Fire
speaking Ballistic Confessions of Truth!

Um hum....
You tried to hit me with your best shot,
but *my* slingshot is suited-up for War.
It is my protection
and direction
bought with perfection
for a few select women on the "front-line!"

No, Don't be mistaken,
this "*Zena Princess Warrior*" is just....
lett'n loose
and embracing all of this "Feisty Divinity"
inside of me.
The more I inhale truth,
the more I achieve.
And as I wipe my wet lips
on my shirt sleeve,
I believe that ...
Greater is.... "the she"
inside of me,
than the she inside of agreements
of fragile success.

See, You don't know me!
And it all because of
my.... Red Kool-aid Stained Tongue!

♣ ♣ ♣ ♣ ♣ ♣ ♣ ♣ ♣ ♣ ♣ ♣

Poem:	*Red Koolaid*
Inspiration:	*written on 09/16/06*
Annotations:	*This poem is my expression as to why I act the way I do lately.*
Dedications:	*To every person that lives their life like the color red with purpose.*
Meditation:	*Proverbs 28:1 "The wicked man flees though no one pursues, but the righteous are as bold as a lion."* *Isaiah 41:10 "Fear not, for I am with you"*
Contemplations:	*Ask Yourself → What keeps you from living your life to the fullest potential?*
	Ask Yourself → What are you truly grounded in about who you are?
	Ask Yourself → What color is your Koolaid?

FLOWERS IN MY SOUL

Tulips,
Lavender,
Dandelions,
Daisy's,
Carnations,
Baby's Breath,
and the Royal Rose.
Just notice how they poise,
and catch your senses.
Fuzzy-Velvet petals collecting tear-drops of rain,
Dancing around in my heart,
It's eye candy,
Hence they capture my nose,
with their sweet smell'n aroma's.
Peace! ... scented with life's simplicities.

Flowers in my soul.
Just notice how they poise
and catch your senses.

Daylilies ... waking up my passions,
Bursting to live on purpose.
Orange and bright,
ready to fight for a life full of....
Red Roses,
standing confident and bold
against the thorns of life's lessons.
Lessons repeated
and lessons learned.

Baby's Breath ...
innocent and lack of knowing
how to avoid the theft and deceiver,
Ready to convert my beige halo into ...
A Wild Flower.
Am I free?
Or Am I lost? ...
in this field of Diverse Stupidity.
I need to find my mentor
who has her own distinct strength.
Besides, there's only one of me
who is uniquely all of me.

Like a Sunflower
reaching for the Sun's warmth,
and reaching for the Son for growth,
I need to see pass the limitations of the weeds,
and the synthetic flowers
in this poppy field of life.

Now, I'm scared like a pink Carnation,
and I'm risking starvation.
I'm only noticed on special occasions,
Delivering a safe smile
and worldly wish for happiness.

I'm bored with pink,
pink carnations stink,
And now I want to sink
into my mink and be a Classy Orchid.
Strutting my scent across this room,
Wanting so badly to be noticed and chosen to love.

But Orchid season comes and goes,
like the sneeze in my allergy nose.

Now finally,
I can feel the petals between my toes,
Relaxed, soft, fertile soil
for me to plant my roots.
I want to be....
just me,
you see.
Blue ... Lavender ... Calm.
Sturdy and upright like a palm.
Now I'm noticed by the Father above,
I've surrendered to Him my hurts and woes,
And my "purple-blue-hues"
are like incense to His nose.

He Loves me,
He loves me not,
He *(my Heavenly Father)*—definitely—Loves—Me!

Flowers in my Soul,
Just notice how they poise and catch your senses.

Hue's of Blue from the summer's dew
reflect His plans of continuous blooms for you,
Just notice the Flowers.

Poem: *Flowers in my Soul*

Inspiration: *written on 05/05/05*

Annotations: *I love flowers and gardens so I thought I'd write a poem about my personality as related to the characters of different flowers.*

Dedications: *My gratitude to God for all the beautiful flowers that scale this Earth .*

Meditation: *Psalms 103:15 "As for man, his days are like grass, he flourishes like a flower of the field;"*
Song of Solomon 2:1 "I am a rose of Sharon, a lily of the valleys."
Isaiah 35:1 "The desert and the parched land will be glad; the wilderness will rejoice and blossom. Like the crocus, ..."

Contemplations: *Ask Yourself* → *What flower would best describe your personality and why?*

Ask Yourself → *What kinds of things help you to remember to stop and smell the roses?*

Ask Yourself → *What's your favorite color of flower and why?*

PROMISE

The other night, I was sitt'n back....
head propped against my pillow
And my closed-eyes rested
in this daydream called "Promise."
It reminded me to....
not treat life like
a crap game or lottery ticket.
See, I'm the only one that knows,
what's been audibly spoken to my heart.
And in this idle imagination,
his faceless grace
carries peace around my ora,
And every pore sweats with passion,
in this easy-going pace with destiny.
I heed to the supreme voice by choice,
as I "live out" my truth fearlessly.
See, "Ol Skool" is unstoppable
with what I'm ground in.
And now, here we are,
having this conversation,
And my truth telling tongue
needs to say,
1st of all,
to all you men,
that tried to prance your glance
in my direction,
now you know,
your game was not authentic.
And so, It's a new day,
and a—*Real*-Brother has found,

what he deserves,
notice I said "found,"
cause ladies trust me,
most men can sniff-out bound-up desperation,
like the smell of "dead skunk"
inside the junk of your trunk.
So ladies, here's a tip,
keep yourself fresh.
Yeah, anybody can take 3 baths a day,
paint your toenails,
workout,
and have you hair laid.
But keep yourself fresh.
Body, mind, and spirit.

So, yeah girl,
I had to checked him out first,
√ Background check,

√ credit check,

√ family check,

√ baby mama-drama check,

√ HIV test,

√ girlfriend-patrol,

√ prayed,

√ fasted,
and all the rest,
just to make sure he was whole.
So now, these baby fingers are engaged
in a Purity Vow,
as we lock-in on love

minus the sex.
We press to follow preparation
and not take for granted
the holy grail of communion in this union.
The price has already been paid,
as we prayed to heal,
with little baggage,
cause we both gave up the load
to people who still wanna play games.
See, I have no problem
confess'n my life lessons,
So my question is,
"What's the purpose of this generational crossbreeding?"
Shoot, besides chemistry
and having things in common,
I need to know
before proceeding to blend my spiritual DNA with yours.
Since we play this game called,
"you-Hunter," & "me-Prey,"
I want to know,
what's the mission of possibilities,
as I inherit seed from you,
that my body is ready to nurture?
Besides, if we can't live forever
leaving trails of "Beautiful,"
Hell, what's the point!
See, as his woman to-be,
all I see,.... is him bowing before me,
thanking that inner voice
for the keys to my heart.
And brother,
as my personal priest,

I see you exchanging holy water
to my hands as confirmation that,
As your wife,
I will "Sub" your "Mission,"
quench your ambitions,
and light fire to your ignition.
And I want you to remember,
the only sentence in this "Pre-nup" is,
God made me whole before I met you ...
so, His ammunition of blank shells,
will be *the only* war stories
collected during *this* chapter of my life.
See ladies,
this man is erect,
upright, and direct,
And he kisses my forehead
as his sister-friend, & mother superior.
Now.... I'm not saying
my new mother-in-law is anything inferior,
but don't get it twisted,
I am his new flavor of estrogen,
whose subliminal duty is to
draw his mind to nothing but
"peaceful" "high-spirited" "fantasies!"
You feel me?
So brother,
like kin,
you redeemed me from a world of singleness.
Yes, I was set-apart,
but never lonely.
So baby,
our kinship has nothing to do with

you bringing me things that I long for.
And I expect your essence
to sharpen my being,
direct my dreams,
and confirm plans *already spoken* to me.
And as my husband-to-be,
I want you to know,
I love you cause
you are a trusted messenger.
And before we open our eyes
to consummate these vows,
braided together,
I'm speaking things as if they were,
and the forecast reads,
you are a suitable husband
for this place called Tami-land.
So I demand that we continuously expand
our love and tent-pegs
as this new journey begins.
Honey, I want you to know,
you bring solace to my soul.
So baby, let's ... let the story unfold.

Poem:	*Promise*
Inspiration:	*written 03/05/07*
Annotations:	*I wrote this poem speaking to the way I see a true loving relationship happening for single women, including me.*
Dedications:	*Promises that will come in time.*
Meditation:	*Proverbs 4:25-27 "Let thine eyes look right on, and let thine eyelids look straight before thee. Ponder the path of*

thy feet, and let all thy ways be established. Turn not to the right hand nor to the left: remove thy foot from evil."

<u>*Luke 12:29-31*</u> *"And seek not ye what ye shall eat, or what ye shall drink, neither be ye of doubtful mind. For all these things do the nations of the world seek after: and your Father knoweth that ye have need of these things. But rather seek ye the kingdom of God; and all these things shall be added unto you."*

Contemplations:

Ask Yourself ➔ *What's more important to you, what you have or what you want?*

Ask Yourself ➔ *Is there any place where life controls you?*

Ask Yourself ➔ *What does having a significant other mean to you?*

GRATITUDE'S ATTITUDE

Gratitude's
Attitude
Harvests
a Heartbeat of
Thankfulness

I LOVE YOU SOUP

This is *not* canned soup, a cup of soup, or dried noodle soup.
This is "I Love You, Soup"

Yes, scoops and scoops of love for the troops,
longing to be fed a heavenly meal.
Lavish upon the feast and see its longing to serve you,
seeking to give, the kind of food that sticks to your ribs,
a kiss from the spoon ready to commune very soon its love for you.

Love, dressed-up for taste-buds that fit the unity of the race.
A broth-base with a chase of potatoes, tomatoes, and split peas that
embrace the bay-leaves and chili pepper.
Okra with Chicken in a bowl,
continuously warms your stomach in cruise-control.

Your heart will loose a load,
as the Love from this soup takes control.
Not too cold and not too hot,
just the right temperature in the slow-cooker's pot.
Just console with the ingredients,
the right shot, of trueloves knot,
and a little salt, hits the right spot.

This is ... "I Love You, Soup"

The Aroma's of turnip bottoms I perceive minus the leaves,
kiss my nose with the abyss of Agape's Love Rose.
Beloved thinks, ponders, and knows your vitamin deficiencies.
The kind of lima beans, broccoli cuts, parsley, onion,
carrots and green-beans to season-up.
Perfection's aroma speaks adoration and envelops me,

patrolling my soul,

I'm free to take in that sea of forgetfulness.

He is "I Love You Soup"

Am I the container for you to pour in your unconditional
affirmations?

I hear your percolating bubbles, giggling, and humming,

the soft clashing wood against the stainless steel.

I'm ready for this meal from the Potter's grill.

Now our connection is a reflection of your song of perfection

leading me in the direction of the section of the kitchen called "The
Stove."

I Love you Soup,

Has **us** face-to-face as my heart is racing to a pace full of Gods grace,

and I feel the mist & steam, upstream hoover over me as the redeemer
beams in.

And I know with my knower, your broth will fulfill my longings.

Cause, I see nutritious swirls and baptized whirlpools of unconditional
love ...

to die for.

And before the spoon kisses my lips,

My heart knows that,

I Love you, because you 1st Loved me.

Sweet quiet slurps, I wrap the swallow around my heart,

Yes, the real part that's fed, as you impart and restart my hunger pains
with,

"I'm full."

And I taste and see that you are Good.

Because you are: "I Love you, Soup"

Poem:	*I Love you Soup*
Inspiration:	*written on 11/02/05*

Annotations: *When you fall in Love with Jesus you will find it to be as delicious as a good warm bowl of soup on a cold lonely day.*

Dedications: *To all the women who participated in the bible study group where we studied a book entitled "Falling in Love with Jesus: Abandoning yourself to the greatest Love of your life."*

Meditation: *Job 22:21-22 "Acquaint now thyself with him, and be at peace: thereby good shall come unto thee. Receive, I pray thee, the law from his mouth, and lay up his words in thine heart."*

Psalms 16:7 "I will bless the LORD, who hath given me counsel: my reins also instruct me in the night seasons.

Proverbs 3:5-6 "Trust in the LORD with all thine heart; and lean not unto thine own understanding. In all thy ways acknowledge him, and he shall direct thy paths."

Jude 1:21 "Keep yourselves in the love of God, looking for the mercy of our Lord Jesus Christ unto eternal life."

Contemplations: *Ask Yourself → What's Love got to do with it?*

Ask Yourself → How do you give and receive Love?

Ask Yourself → Who have you fallen in Love with and how did it make you feel?

IT'S JUST FAMILIAR

My Mother, my sister, and home girl too.
The connection happens immediately
like two beads of water on
a fogged mirror of yesterday.
I see the eyes to her soul
and her voice is a familiar Echo.
She knows *(She knows)*,
I know *(I know)*,
We know *(We know)*,
One God, One Spirit—
Captured in a Glance!

The fight has numbed me,
but I look beyond my weary thoughts,
and the Kati-corners of confusion on this road.
She passes the torch in a blink-of-an-eye,
then slowly opens with a gentle smile.
Stormy life lessons
is the wrinkle above the brow.
One God, One Spirit—
Captured in a Glance!

My Student-Mentor,
like mirrors facing an endless reflection.
Her hug is from the inside out.
I can feel her strength
like the waves of labor pains.
I know the shadow of tomorrow's wisdom is upon me.

Deep in those eyes.... down deep,
I remember the life before.

The glance is over.
She knows *(She knows)*,
I know *(I know)*,
We know *(We know)*,
We will see each other in the life to come,
One God, One Spirit—
Captured in a Glance!
It's all Good,
It's Just,
Familiar.

Poem:	*It's Just Familiar*
Inspiration:	*written on 03/07/02*
Annotations:	*I wrote this about one year before my mother lost her battle with cancer.*
Dedications:	*To my mother, who was an incredibly strong, witty, loving, feisty, and comical person. She modeled being a strong, intelligent, independent woman to me. It was God's purpose for her to be my mother.*
Meditation:	*Genesis 48:4 "And said unto me, Behold, I will make thee fruitful, and multiply thee, and I will make of thee a multitude of people; and will give this land to thy seed after thee for an everlasting possession."*
	Psalms 90:2 "Before the mountains were brought forth, or ever thou hadst formed the earth and the world, even from everlasting to everlasting, thou art God."
Contemplations:	*Ask Yourself → What will the two dashes between your tombstone mean to the people that knew you? What contributions and story will you leave behind after you die?*

3 JEWELS

Pure, Resilient, Strong, & Feminine.
3 Jewels fashioned by God's Brilliance.
Just gaze into their spirits,
they sparkle with Peace, Joy, & Smiles.
3 Jewels
3 Jewels
In Mama's Jewelry Box.
3 Jewels with their ancestral layers pressed together
like rings of an old olive tree.
Amethyst.... passionately purple.
Topaz ... serene bluish green.
and my Pearl ... calm swirls of opaque cream.
3 Jewels.
Mama's smooth skinned, sweet smelling rocks.
Bellied-up from the mineral earth of my being.
Yes, I sharpened and shaped their surfaces
with my Diamond shaped hands.
Washed in water and polished by life's lessons.
Priceless gifts, yes they are priceless!
My 3 Jewels,
My Ashleigh,
My Tyler,
My Paige.

Poem:	*3 Jewels*
Inspiration:	*written on 03/30/01*
Annotations:	*I wrote this with my children in mind; Children are a gift from God. But when my children aren't acting like pre-*

cious gift, I read this poem to them in their purest form. Yes, meaning when they were innocent little sweet smelling babies. Okay I'm venting cause they are teenagers as I write this book. (smiles)

Dedications:

To Ashleigh, Tyler, and Paige

Meditation:

<u>Exodus 20:12</u> *"Honour thy father and thy mother: that thy days may be long upon the land which the LORD thy God giveth thee."*

<u>Deuteronomy 6:6-9</u> *"And these words, which I command thee this day, shall be in thine heart: And thou shalt teach them diligently unto thy children, and shalt talk of them when thou sittest in thine house, and when thou walkest by the way, and when thou liest down, and when thou risest up. And thou shalt bind them for a sign upon thine hand, and they shall be as frontlets between thine eyes. And thou shalt write them upon the posts of thy house, and on thy gates."*

Contemplations:

Ask Yourself➔ What's young-hearted about you?

Ask Yourself➔ Is there any value in being young-hearted? Why or Why not?

Ask Yourself➔ Has a child ever taught you anything very valuable? If so, what and why was it valuable?

MY'Z CHICAGO PEOPLES

Smooth Roasted Amber, Brownish Bronze,
Barbequed Vanilla Pecans,
truffles of café au leit swirls,
and those Sepia Brazilian tones.
We are the Chocolate Rainbow's promise
to never drown-out the Genetic Strain with
triple-K Activities or Genocide Festivities,
because you see, once you turn "Brown"
you don't drown in the noun called "Racial Self-Hate."

I love *My peoples*,
the kinds that laugh & entertain themselves,
with Kool-Aid Sips,
sardines on a cracker,
and Sitt'n in that folded lawn chair.
Play'n some "Ooh that's my song" in the backdrop.
Every shape & hue, muscle & curve,
some smart, and some without a clue.
My peoples be un-glued from the judgments of this World,
free to flirt, look you up and down & roll their eyes.
I just smile and bat my eyes in "Aw"
of how we be roll'n-up, style'n and profile'n.
Yeah, we like run'n our bizinesses,
push'n politics, gett'n educated & degreed,
Breed'n our children to take Jesus as their Lead.
Embracing our ethnicity with
colly-greens, kente cloths, & beauty-aids.
Mastering some great athletic things,
unapologetic, yes <u>we </u>have the genetics
minus the synthetics to master things like

the fight in boxing,
running track for survival,
or Dancing God's Grace in Broadway's theatrics.
Free to wear our hair natural,
waves of braids, locks, & curly twisted-Plats.
Pressed, permed, and weaved,
shiny, in shades of purple to hot orange & green.
I just love *My Chicago Peoples* ...
their boldness to stretch beyond the norm.
We instinctively reach beyond ordinary,
in search of that inner artistic voice.
Strive'n to tap-dance with the Spirit of Abstract,
Unpaintable Choreography,
and Life's Rendering Realism.
We Believe so we can achieve ourselves.
We politely Nod
as we pass each other on the street,
acknowledging God's light in each other,
yes, a priceless glance & smile
from God's grand land of Dark-Brown-Cushites.
Our continuous fight
to be respected & treated right
is the insightful concern,
but the pitiful rights for the person called bigot,
who never learned to appreciate the color wheels
"earth tones" in the great Crayola box of 48.
My Peoples,
be free, speak'n our own dialect of language,
intentionally divided in the Master's Plan
to reach the heartbeat of family & friends.
See, the essence of Love really sweats down to your pores,
your brown hues speak sonnets in holy lands.

We are a pure poetic verse
from the Chocolate Rainbow's Reflection.
So, respect the interconnection of iridescent complexions
and take kindly to the one who painted you with perfection.
My Peoples ... just pause and refresh yourself,
because *You Are* Beautifully Loved!
You are My'z Peoples.

♣ ♣ ♣ ♣ ♣ ♣ ♣ ♣ ♣ ♣ ♣ ♣

Poem:	*My'z Peoples*
Inspiration:	*written on 07/06/06*
Annotations:	*I wrote this on an airplane coming from my home town, Chicago.*
Dedications:	*To my brown-skinned brothas and sistahs in Chicago.*
Meditation:	<u>*Romans 14:19*</u> *"Let us therefore follow after the things which make for peace, and things wherewith one may edify another.*
	<u>*1 Corinthians 14:26*</u> *"How is it then, brethren? when ye come together, every one of you hath a psalm, hath a doctrine, hath a tongue, hath a revelation, hath an interpretation. Let all things be done unto edifying."*
Contemplations:	*Ask Yourself* → *How much do you love the skin you're in? Is it vanity or love?*
	Ask Yourself → *How much do you love or dislike other colors of skin? Why?*

LAMB & BEEF ON A STICK

Crumbs on the table,
and I sit here in thought
about my 1st Gyros sandwich,
shared with my non-Greek boyfriend.
High school date food,
he paid my way
and enjoyed watching me
eat his hard earned money.
30 years later,
its memory still taste like
the 1st kiss we had.
Comfort food,
not careful about eating with manners,
Just us …
being hungry for fun
and lots of ketchup to skirt on French fries.
My eyes sparkled
in the reflection of those 1970's sun glasses,
masking the koolness
of him being my boyfriend.
6 feet tall
greeting me daily in his baby-blue Maverick,
always clean
with stereo sounds from backseat speakers
grooving to the mist of
fogged mirrors after long kisses.
Yes, Gyros meat
still stuck between his teeth and mine,
Flossing was out of site
because all we wanted *to be* was

"Always and forever."
Him courting me,
and me feeling like a princess
he chose to ask,
Yes, he was scared at first
like Black pepper,
so he asked his good friend …
to ask me instead,
but you know what I said,
If my non-Greek boyfriend
wants a date with me,
he'll have to ask me himself, you see.
So he did.
And here I am
having this memory
of my 1st Gyros sandwich on a date,
and it's a great memory
that I will never erase.
Cause I'm sitting here
at "Falafel King" all alone,
and they're cutting me some of that
Lamb and Beef that's shaped like a cone,
roasting on a vertical rotisserie grill.

Poem:	*Lamb and Beef on a Stick*
Inspiration:	*written on 04/16/07*
Annotations:	*Just a stream of consciousness I was having at Lunch-time.*
Dedications:	*To my 1st boyfriend, Michael, who took me on my 1st date as a teenager.*

Meditation:	<u>2 Corinthians 9:11</u> *"Being enriched in every thing to all bountifulness, which causeth through us thanksgiving to God."*
	<u>Ephesians 5:20</u> *"Giving thanks always for all things unto God and the Father in the name of our Lord Jesus Christ;"*
Contemplations:	*Ask Yourself* ➔ *What small thing have you given God thanks for lately?*
	Ask Yourself ➔ *Are you eating and choosing your food wisely?*
	Ask Yourself ➔ *What's your comfort food and why?*

JUST NOTICE

Just Notice
and
Appreciate
the
Gifts
in the *Garden* of Life

I REMEMBER

I remember being a little girl,
noticing the butterflies landing on the green, thick grass.
I remember that dogs were stinky and had bad breath.
All the big trees and how they peaked through the branches,
the smell of summer, autumn leaves, and rainy-day worms.
The smell of stinky-wet dogs, and thick smoke from the fireplace Log.
I remember the basement had cinder blocks and concrete floors.
My sister and I use to roller skate around that steel pole like
    roller-derby.
I remember mini-skirts, go-go boots, converses, hot pants & the
    Jackson 5.
My mother dressing us alike, my first 10-speed bike,
and the sound of the Ice-cream truck.
I remember Frozen Kool-aid in a Dixie cup,
drinking from that green water hose,
hot humid days, as we played for endless hours in front of the house,
double-Dutch, hand-clapping games, jacks, and Chinese jump rope.
I remember saying "Sike-Yo-Mind" & "Gimmie-Five,"
and that our next-door neighbor was the snitching-kind.
I remember playing Dodge-ball & Red-Rover with the kids on the
    block,
cod-liver oil, chamomile lotion, and kids with chicken pox.
We had to come in when the streetlights came on,
raking leaves, cutting grass, & swinging on the weeping willow tree
    out back.
I remember Daddy painting the house, barbequing that stack of ribs,
Mama checking my homework and her new Afro-Wig.
Boston Bake Beans, Dixie sticks, and pickle with a peppermint inside,
and people would wear peace signs on their neck with pride.
I remember going to church, kneel & pray, holy water,
and the confession booth seemed like everyday.

I remember that I wanted to be a Nun ...
yeh, I know, that lasted for about 7 days,
when I realized that the "Flying Nun Show"
was just little girls "Super-Hero" phase.
I remember that ugly brown & beige uniform,
and those red, yellow & green tye-dyed tea shirts,
Halloween parties, Christmas caroler's,
and the invention of down-feather coats.
Baby dolls that wet their pants and paper snow flakes,
Hot wheel cars, and knitting my first scarf.
I remember Daddy singing along with
Nat King Cole, Marvin Gaye, and those Sinatra tones like
"Fly me to the Moon!"
You could simply scare someone by just saying "Boo!"
You could take a nap at noon, with the door wide open,
yes we had it made in the shade.
I use to sleep on the top bunk and stare at the blue-painted ceiling,
& see the stars through the cracked window shade as the night would
     fade.
I remember hearing the wind blow at night,
and the hallow sounds of the trains passing by.
I remember hash & eggs, grits, and toast, sweet potato pie & pot roast.
Daddy calling us by our nicknames,
and me calling by brothers and sister by their not-so-nice nicknames.
I remember going shopping with my mother & sister, begging for
     stuff,
and my mother saying, I don't think so cause you have enough.
Goldblatts, Woolworth, and Sears were the shopping havens,
I remember fighting my sister over wearing my new blouse & coat,
and the first time I puffed a cigarette that burnt my throat.
Vaseline on your legs, and wearing blue eye-shadow to school,
my sister fought my first fight for me and how I became instantly kool.

I remember doing my chores 5 minutes before my Mama got home,
station wagons, Beatles, Black & White TV, and the Afro-pic Comb.
I remember Batman, Green Acres, Petty-Coat Junction,
& Creature-Feature at night, Drive-Inn's movies,
a bucket of chicken, and jiffy-pop popcorn, and flying a kite.
I remember Red Kool-aid, French fries, ketchup & old grease.
My cousin's ballet recital, and Aunt Saundra's Apple tree.
Daddy Roger's laugh & Grandfathers raspy voice,
my Grandmother pressing my hair … and burning me.
I remember the smell of the straitening comb on the stove,
and the sweet potato pie too,
Foot prints of my child-hood are safe and free,
Given to me by the ones before me, you see,
So, I thank God that I have a lot to remember.
And I question myself and you as well,
What will you leave behind to remember & tell?

Poem:	*I Remember*
Inspiration:	*written on 04/09/01*
Annotations:	*Flashback in time … Ol' Skool Style.*
Dedications:	*To my siblings, Staci, Tony, & Kelly.*
Meditation:	<u>*Deuteronomy 4:9-10*</u> *"Only take heed to thyself, and keep thy soul diligently, lest thou forget the things which thine eyes have seen, and lest they depart from thy heart all the days of thy life: but teach them thy sons, and thy sons' sons; Specially the day that thou stoodest before the LORD thy God in Horeb, when the LORD said unto me, Gather me the people together, and I will make them hear my words, that they may learn to fear me all the days that they shall live upon the earth, and that they may teach their children."*

Contemplations: *Ask Yourself* ➐ *What stories will you leave behind for your nieces, nephews, grandchildren, and great grandchildren?*

SPIRIT HIKE

I'm here!
and You are around me,
I feel your breath and close my eyes
and see the *Silent-Presence* of you.
Lime green, sage green,
stone white, and rusty pink.
I hear your creations all around me,
the little bird with the loud voice.
The buzzing fly,
the whistle of the wind
and the blue-painted sky.
I see straw yellow grass,
growing between the rocks.
There is life after death in this sea of rocks.
The sun is behind me peaking over my shoulder.
A small moth just floated and danced with wind,
I see why the You visit here again and again.
I see moss growing between the ant mountains,
lime moss, brown moss and salt stains,
yes, I see left-over drops of rain.
I see sand grooves you carved with your hands,
blue sky, white cotton clouds,
and *Silence Echo's Out-Loud*.
There are hidden treasures and unseen creatures,
peaking and reaching for light.
This feels edible,
like the lick of an ice cube.
And it's nourishing because it's still flourishing.
Edible, cold, cool, soft and rough.
Conforming, sculpted, rigid, fine detailed lines of Art.

Each plant You instructed to be named
because none are the same.
There's peace in my spirit that I can't explain.
I long to travel from place to place to be with you,
yet You're with me, in me, through me, because you knew me.
Combing my hair and touching me with a kiss of fresh sunshine.
This is Why ...
I thank you for Silence, Solitude
and the warmth against my skin,
The wind cools my pores,
and the truth about You is where I begin.
God in this time
you have reminded me that you made me in your image.
Thank you for this moment of time to **honor You in Solitude**.

Poem:	*Spirit Hike*
Inspiration:	*written on 08/11/02*
Annotations:	*I wrote this piece while on my 1ˢᵗ real vacation with no kids accompanying me. This also happen to be at Snow Cap Canyon, UT with seven of my girlfriends who were turning 40'ish. It was a great adventure spa vacation.*
Dedications:	*To my 30+10'ish girlfriends who I had so much fun with; I truly cherish our friendships.*
Meditation:	*Colossians 4:2 "Continue in prayer, and watch in the same with thanksgiving;"*
	Matthew 6:5-12 "And when thou prayest, thou shalt not be as the hypocrites are: for they love to pray standing in the synagogues and in the corners of the streets, that they may be seen of men. Verily I say unto you, They have their reward. But thou, when thou prayest, enter into thy closet, and when thou hast shut thy door, pray to thy Father

which is in secret; and thy Father which seeth in secret shall reward thee openly. But when ye pray, use not vain repetitions, as the heathen do: for they think that they shall be heard for their much speaking. Be not ye therefore like unto them: for your Father knoweth what things ye have need of, before ye ask him. After this manner therefore pray ye: Our Father which art in heaven, Hallowed be thy name. Thy kingdom come, Thy will be done in earth, as it is in heaven. Give us this day our daily bread. And forgive us our debts, as we forgive our debtors."

Contemplations:

Ask Yourself ➔ *How do the words Solitude, Aloneness, Isolation, and Solitary make you feel? And Why?*

Ask Yourself ➔ *What does true relaxation look like to you?*

Ask Yourself ➔ *When was the last time you did something "Just Because?" What was it and how did it make you feel?*

OCTOBER GRATITUDE

Weeping willows sway,
wet puppies, autumn leaves and humming birds.
The season of thick sounds,
bright smells,
and cozy soft blankets.
Ummmmm!
The cool cold air against my legs,
I'm wearing my plaid skirt today.
My nose is red
and my fingers tingle like peppermint.
Ahhh!
I can see my breath and feel my ears.
I think I'll search the grass for a 3-leaf clover.
Wow!!! they taste like lemons.
I smell orange peels
and see cracked pecan shells
and those funny shaped squash on the coffee table.
Oooh!! the sun is orange
and the stars are reachable.
Let's catch a lightening bug.
I feel like spittin' pomegranate seeds
and eatin' a Carmel apple.
Pumpkin fills the air.
The sound of crickets and dogs howling
against the dark blue midnight sky.
Yarn for hand-knit mitten
and bifocals by the seat cushion.
Flag-stoned walkways
led me to that cup of cinnamon flavored
hot apple cider.

Yes, the cloudy rusty kind.
Fresh crisp sounds of leaves falling
and popcorn popping.
Fireplace hibernation is in the air.
The smell of burnt wood,
foggy piers,
quiet oceans
and roasted chestnuts.
Strings of holiday lights,
long walks and pine trees.
Fallen acorns,
squirrels and rainy day worms fill the air
with the smell of wet leaves and muddy puddles.
I need my yellow rain coat
and rubber boots.
Think I'll write a letter on this faded paper.
Clean the garage and rake the leaves.
Need my cutout gloves
to cover my cracked dry hands.
Dirty fingernails,
it's time to plant my tulips
and trim my bushes.
Sweep the walkway
and pickup broken tree branches.
Damp jeans,
football games
and candle-lit dinners.
Cornbread, beef stew, chili,
and grandma's wooden spoon
stirring the cast-iron kettle.
Bay leaves, dried flowers, red roses
and lilac ground cover.

My flannel pajamas have hole in the butt,
I feel a breeze.
I want to paint my toenails
fire engine red
while I blend a little
Black & White TV in.
October is like a cup of
sleepy-time tea
with a chase of
Peaceful thoughts.
My Heavenly Father,
I thank you for October.

♣ ♣ ♣ ♣ ♣ ♣ ♣ ♣ ♣ ♣ ♣ ♣

Poem:	*October Gratitude*
Inspiration:	*written on 10/09/01*
Annotations:	*Being grateful for the small things and knowing that the small things are really the big things.*
Dedications:	*To all of my nature-lovin, tree-huggin' friends.*
Meditation:	*Genesis 1:1-31 "In the beginning God created the heaven and the earth...."(a lots more to read.... open the Bible please.)*
Contemplations:	*Ask Yourself → What are you grateful for?*
	Ask Yourself → What's your favorite season? And Why?

Hmmmm!

Hmmmm!
Reflections
&
Meditations
Water my
Poetic
Dedication

THE SUM OF ALL POEMS

Just imagine, in your *Dying* hour, the sirens have rung, oxygen pumps through your hands, and you *can still* harmonize words holding the pen....

If you could write one *last Poem* telling God what you felt about your time here on earth, what would you *write*? ... Your last assignment is a 3-minute Abstract Vocal Vitae for Heavens auditory eardrum. So how will you *flow* for the audience of Angelic spectators: like grandma, big daddy, auntie and them? What will you say opening night at the Holy City's curtain rising on the picture screen show featuring "Uniquely You?"

I see the clock ticks, and I have 59 minutes left, the paper sucks the ink gripping every swirl and curve like the dips of a roller coaster, wanting to scream & holler-out, because I lived in & out most of the visions in my minds-eye. On this journey, yes, my *indecisions* & fears delayed my stepping into the mapped-out plan of *precision* for me, but I'm glad you navigated me through cold sweats of emotional-worry that I would fail at being "uniquely me." **Thank You**, Brave Beginner, my founder who established all, & on the 7th day you rested, because you loaded me with all the bells and whistles.

The clock ticks, and I see 40 minutes are left, my pen has rhythmic sounds like swirls of soft whistles drumming echoes of urgency to capture only the things that really matter. You see I want to write about where I went, solitude, & what *You* rescued me from. But somehow, I imagine yawning moments, I want to nullify any instances where arms-fold, eyes close, or those "chagrin-type smiles" plastered on faces. What shall I pronounce as my "line of verse", my sonnet, my rhythmic pattern of Rumbatic, Salsa, the heart-beat dance of my earthly life? What shall I write?

The Clock ticks, and 30 minutes are left, I pause to laugh, nervously ... pen between thumb & pointer, pivoting like a fast-motion see-saw. Making sounds like humming birds & karate sticks. Whisking the air, I bite, leaving my teeth prints, baring down to capture only the essence of frankincense and myrrh. I toil to dispense things that make sense. Not excuses of suspense, like I had a flat tire, that's why I had nothing to write. I want to showcase obedience without pretense. How I danced with gratitude, laughter, along with my prissy attitude, & opened doors to see new days as great days ... before my shadow ceased to exist in this matrix called the 21st Century. And I pause to realize that some will, and some won't, make the opening night at the theatre in the sky.

The Clock ticks, 12 minutes are left: Time is flashing fast-forward, dashing past me, like the 12 tribes of African and European blood that flows through me, pro-creating Kings, Priest, & Queens feasting on daily manna. The drumbeat of "thirsty hope" bombards my gates, my pearls, & the keepers guarding my heavenly Estate. Suited-up swinging my "razor sharp" sword of kindness, as a brave Lioness, I was redeemed by your perfect Love. Yes, like the 12, "I to," was **Droppin' Seeds**, Watering helpless weeds, Feed'n the earths dirt, with the dessert called prayer iced in amazing grace, and I hope the pace of my race was worth *another* promotion in the place called, timeless existence. I truly adore you Jesus.

The Clock ticks, and I have 3 minutes left I hear the reel of the tape approaching its completion, And I scurry to pluck-off my heart, all tumble weeds, the prickly, thorny, ill-natured acts, have been the toughest to resist. But my childhood quiet has birthed an extroverted loquacious, mouth-piece ... passionate to pop up like jack-in-the box, to speak that freeing truth, so as you know there was no stoppin' me. Me, like aged wine, un-blinded by pride, I learned to forgive, walk away, pray, hold my tongue, dismay hateful grudges, so you would dismiss my hurts and I honor your greatness. I stand before you, to say again, I Love you, Father.

The Clock ticks, and 1 minute is left: My left-handed wrist flicks to cross all T's and dot all I's. And as I leave behind everything *that's not* on this paper, I breath deep to Kiss the memories with, at last, I understand that you cashed-in on an exchange to have complete Unity with me and I'm really ready, yes ready, to meet up with you again.

So Writers, Poets, and Literary Giants, I'll see ya at the theatre in the sky & I really hope you have a ticket ... oh yeah, one other thing, your tickets were all pre-purchased.

Poem: *The Sum of all Poems*

Inspiration:	*written on 04/10/06*
Annotations:	*My account to God one day.*
Dedications:	*To all Poets, Literary Giants, Anonymous Writers, and Lyricist.*
Meditation:	*Proverbs 18:21 "Death and life are in the power of the tongue: and they that love it shall eat the fruit thereof."*
	Romans 12:3-8 "For I say, through the grace given unto me, to every man that is among you, not to think of himself more highly than he ought to think; but to think soberly, according as God hath dealt to every man the measure of faith. For as we have many members in one body, and all members have not the same office: So we, being many, are one body in Christ, and every one members one of another. Having then gifts differing according to the grace that is given to us, whether prophecy, let us prophesy according to the proportion of faith; Or ministry, let us wait on our ministering: or he that teacheth, on teaching; Or he that exhorteth, on exhortation: he that giveth, let him do it with simplicity; he that ruleth, with diligence; he that sheweth mercy, with cheerfulness."
Contemplations:	*Ask Yourself → Do the words that come out of your mouth well thought out most of the time?*
	Ask Yourself → What gift, talents, and abilities do you possess and are using to your fullest ability?
	Ask Yourself → If you're not using them, what's holding you back?

NO SMILES

Thoughts of
Black & White photos from the olden days.
Sepia Brown, Tea-stained, faded cracked paper,
and a blurred haze outlines the profiles of glassy tears.
The wind is still and the flash from the antique camera
know nothing about red-eye.

BUT WHY, NO SMILES?

A Snap-shot of Hard Work, Yellow eyes, hidden despair,
and handcuffed longings to "Just-be" an-existing-human.
Sleepwalking trance, working the Railroad, Farming cotton,
and Squatting to have 12 babies.
The look on their faces *silence my thoughts.*
Yet their attire is perfectly coordinated.
Ruffles, dusty black suits, petticoats, and ribbons in hair.
Sunday's best, the family keepsake,
passed to the upper pocket of a soldier's coat.
Grandma pearls, sacks of chewing tobacco,
button-up boots, corsets, chastity belts, pockets watches,
cast iron skillets, open fires,
and wooden spoons stirring to feed the family's hunger pains.

BUT IF YOU LOOK REALLY CLOSE ...

I suppose you'll See a hint of tea-rose
on the cheeks of even on the brownish child.
Plump *Pomegranate-stained* Lips....
grip the hidden smile of Freedom ... Hoped-For.
Truth ... "all-knowing"
down in the core

with the tenacity of an unleashed Lion …
Yes, it flows through their veins.
The greatness of God
lurks between the muscle of hard work,
bloody knuckles and bruised knees
as they pray for a life without strife.

And WITH NO SMILES,
THEIR EYES SPEAK "HOPE" **_TO THE NEXT GENERATION._**

Poem:	*No Smiles*
Inspiration:	*written on 9/28/05*
Annotations:	*Inspiration: I was looking at an old Photo, didn't know the people in the photo, but I could still seem to understand who they were.*
Dedications:	*To my ancestors before me.*
Meditation:	<u>*Psalms 33:18-22*</u> *"Behold, the eye of the LORD is upon them that fear him, upon them that hope in his mercy; To deliver their soul from death, and to keep them alive in famine. Our soul waiteth for the LORD: he is our help and our shield. For our heart shall rejoice in him, because we have trusted in his holy name. Let thy mercy, O LORD, be upon us, according as we hope in thee.*
Contemplations:	*Ask Yourself → What does "Hope" mean to you?*
	Ask Yourself → What are you hoping for?
	Ask Yourself → What do you desire in life?

I SEE TRAIN TRACKS

Morality,....
Meditation, ...
and then comes Wisdom!,
Connected like the stations at a train stop.
Do you know where you're going?....
Because,I see train tracks ahead.
Like a frog on a Lily pad,....
which way do I go?
Are my feet stuck on stupid? ...
Or are my thoughts like
the moves of a Chess Game?
Step-out!,
Step-On!,
and Step-In! ...
your decisions.
Through the Fog and the Smog,
Clearly I see,
the next destination.
A leap of faith,
and a Flicker of light out of Wisdom's Eye,
I move the thoughts of my mind
through my secret funnel.
You See,
many stay behind in Ego-Ville.
There's drama,
distractions,
and sleep-walking tours
on a daily basis there!
Yet, the next stop is DESERTED
and very very STILL.

Some get off,
but all disappear.
It looks like death to the dead,
but it's Life to the spirit that's fed.
It's me and You
and the You inside of me.
And we talk of ways
the are not my own.
Just answer the phone,
listen to My tone.
I'll take you to the zone,
stop your moan!
Jesus will "Love" you
deep-down-to-the-bone.
Yes, I'm staying on this train
to the high road ahead.
Morality was the stop in Ego's-Ville.
Mediation is next,
if you choose your Inner-Will.
Wisdom is the Voice
heard years & miles away.
Passengers that know "Love"
hear its pitch night & day.
The tracks are the path,
and the stops are the stations.
The Fare is the same,
but the Focus is Destination.
Stay connected to the fuel
of Prayer & Meditation.
The Lily pads of Life are there for a Reason.
Just choose to "Love"

during your travel this Season.

... Because, I See Train Tracks Ahead.

Poem:	*I see train tracks*
Inspiration:	*written on 03/21/02*
Annotations:	*Where am I headed in life?*
Dedications:	*To People who are looking forward to the road ahead.*
Meditation:	<u>*Matthew 7:14*</u> *"Because strait is the gate, and narrow is the way, which leadeth unto life, and few there be that find it.*
Contemplations:	*Ask Yourself→ Where are you headed in life?*
	Ask Yourself→ Who's following you?
	Ask Yourself → Are you a role-model (leader) or a follower?

THE GARDEN OF INTIMACY

Umm!
Let's see,
I want to examine the garden inside of me.
Is this a journey?
Or is this a venture?
My garden is changed,
it's not the same.
This place is foreign,
it's not familiar.
For the first time,
I'm excited
when I've always been
unfulfilled.
Grass between my toes,
I feel rested instead of restless.
The sun hits my body
and there's a glow I can't see.
It replaces the gloom
that was all on me.
Ripe, Red, and Round,
instead of
Rotten, Dead, and Brown.
I'm hungry
and everything you feed me
taste so good.
My taste buds are bland
when I'm fed from own hand.
Now, I feel like I should eat to live,
and not live to eat.
I'm alive in God's vision

instead of asleep in my own dream.
Swollen cravings unique to my temple,
versus dehydrated longings
that made the madness so simple.
I like this new place,
my growth is a rapid gestation.
Outside this garden
is an alley of stagnation.
Hold-up, I need to slow down.
My feet are swollen and hot,
because my walk has always been
tied in some knot.
I'm laughing and crying
all in the same breathe,
change is around me
and I'm not scared to death.
Oh look, I can't see my toes,
my fulfillment is in the way,
and its discomfort is better than
the frustrations of yesterday.
Our voices dialog
and echo our love for each other.
I career you and talk to you,
you say I am your child.
I use to look at you and suppress you
so I could talk out loud.
From the tomb to the Temple,
the milk is rich and pure
and not man-made.
It's time, it's time,
my water will burst,
it's that simple.

The sun is hot
and my body sweats beads as I travail.
My world outside this garden
is nothing but a green painted hell.
I use to gasp, but now I pant!
I use to shove, but now I push!
I use to grab, but now I grip!
I can feel this baby passing through my hips!
Things were tense,
but this intense.
Before, I was afraid
but now I fear the power.
10 minutes seem like 10 hours.
The moan of my anguish is gone.
I just bear-down and push,
to hear my own song.
There's a cause for the focus
and not a curse for the cause.
This intimacy with You
has led to a birth without pause.
The Cause.
The Intent
is right under my nose.
Yes, You whispered
you are a brown rose,
and I'm blooming everyday.
And I can be nourished in every way.
Blue Sky,
Green Carpet,
and the voice inside,
makes the brown rose
smell like Heaven's pride.

The experience of the garden
is in each of us,
just close your eyes
and look inside
for
the garden of intimacy.

Poem:	*The Garden of Intimacy*
Inspiration:	*written on 02/18/02, 9:00pm*
Annotations:	*I wrote this as an examination of my intimacy (closeness) with God.*
Dedications:	*To people that continuously want a closer relationship with their maker.*
Meditation:	*John 15:4 "Remain in me, and I will remain in you. No branch can bear fruit by itself; it must remain in the vine. Neither can you bear fruit unless you remain in me."*
Contemplations:	*Ask Yourself* → *Do you know yourself well?*
	Ask Yourself → *How would you describe who you really are down to the core?*
	Ask Yourself → *Do you feel you are sabotaging yourself, in any way?*

OL' SKOOL HAIKU

1.

Spring echo's bird songs
Rusty leaves spiral slowly
New birth pushes up

2.

Labor pains pant hot
Baby sees water no more
The happy belly

3.

Whipped my kids today
Flossed teeth keep grim from creeping
Head clear of clutter

4.

Burning thighs breath life
Heart runs pulse red blood through me
Calories drop fat

Poem:	*Ol' Skool Haiku*
Inspiration:	*written on 03/25/06*
Annotations:	*It is challenging to write short poems since I'm so long winded, so here they are…. Short, Sassy, Haiku.*
Dedications:	*To the art of poetry, Haiku Style.*

978-0-595-43388-9
0-595-43388-X

Made in the USA
Lexington, KY
14 December 2011